We Were Funding China's Growth

That Had To Stop!

And: Chinese Disinformation, Aimed at the American Public.

Edouard Prisse

Contents

Dedication

To my children, Thesa, Caroline, Florent and how we enjoyed living in Baambrugge, this little village not far from Amsterdam, in the Netherlands!

Acknowledgments

I wish to thank Hans van der Steur and his lovely American wife Anne for suggesting me to write this book; Twice UN Security Council President Peter van Walsum (†) for his friendship; Annemieke de Nijs for being the first person to seriously have edited this text; Professor Sander Griffioen for his very useful comments; Nout Wellink, former President of the Dutch National Bank, for allowing discussions where we sometimes differed; pastor Carel ter Linden for listening; my five fine children for their on and off support and finally my friend Gregory Nemes who, at his lovely summer address, reluctantly allowed me to write fanatically while he had expected an entertaining guest. Lovely people all.

About the Author

Mr. Prisse loves the US and wants to help its future. The basis of his writing is his ability to put macro-economics, as explained by John Maynard Keynes, into practice for a solution to our present trade problem.

Foreword

Dear reader, before reading this foreword, I suggest you first go to Chapter 1. It immediately shows you what this book is about, and starting in this way is probably a good idea. Only then come back here, if you want.

In life, one is sometimes handed an unwanted responsibility. I received one of those through two experiences that then made me study our recent economic decisions with China and write this book.

The first of these experiences came in 1990 when, after the fall of the Berlin Wall when, in my Dutch newspaper NRC, I had written that every productive enterprise in the former German Democratic Republic (the GDR) would face bankruptcy—including even all farms.

That seemed obvious as Chancellor Helmuth Kohl had decided the new Eastern provinces, the so-called Länder, would receive the strong West German currency as theirs too. With borders opening to efficient Western Germany, competition for those Easterners, with their inefficient ex-Marxist economy, would become impossible. The strange experience was that nobody else wrote that or explained it, but it so happened. The ensuing human drama – as practically everybody lost their jobs in these new provinces - was ignored by the German government that had just triumphantly moved from Bonn to Berlin. This major economic error was shifted under the carpet.

Then, in 2003, I foresaw the too-fast growth of China, due to its so much lower production costs. Again, I was told I was wrong, but that prediction was correct as well. This too great enrichment is even now happening, and its consequences are doing us in. This is the subject of this book. Again, I was the only one in the West to write this correct prediction.

Both experiences were based on an understanding of macroeconomics that I had acquired decades before, when fanatically studying John Maynard Keynes' 'Theory of Employment'. To my later astonishment, it appeared that I understand the practical usage of this theory better than most scholars, professors and economic advisers in the West.

*****

In 2000 I saw President Bill Clinton initiate free trade with China on totally misconceived arguments, see Chapter 1. So, in 2004, I took up an intense study of economic and political events in our economic relationship with China, and in this book, I try to expose the consequences of President Clinton's error and, as second subject, I suggest what we may still do to correct it.

A Fifth Column.

The third subject of this book is the exposure of a so-called 'fifth column', the still unrecognized secret disinformation activity by Chinese-born scholars in the US.

*****

Whether China will really get the upper hand in the world while we just let that happen or, inversely, the democratic countries together will stand up and take correcting measures against the present growth of Chinese power, that is still unsure. Half-way solutions, like the White House has been adopting in 2024, will certainly continue to fail. Economic and trade advisers under President Biden did not recognize that we, in our free trade with China since the year 2001, are making a huge error. President Trump recently decided on a 245% tariff in Chinese goods!

Now that means he has stopped the existing free trading for incoming Chinese goods. In my opinion, this is wonderful as this almost exactly mirrors what this book suggests, except that The White House's method is chaotic and upsets the stock market and Americans citizens, while the method this book proposes is very well prepared and more deliberate.

One thing is certain, though. Only the US can stop the ongoing damage, the European Union cannot. Far worse than what we see in the US, in Brussels, there is a total lack of economic insight and even attention to China's upcoming power. The warning in this book is, therefore, meant for the US, but not just for every clear-thinking American who wants to know about our future. It is also meant for the advisers to the White House, in order to help them see what their predecessors have been so dangerously shortsighted about.

In the course of his first presidency, Mr. Trump showed he understands China's economic danger. President Biden, while

3

clearly understanding the military threat from China, did not understand the economic one.

Meanwhile, the best American professional to know how to tackle this economic problem is arguably diplomat Rober E. Lighthizer, a former adviser to President Trump about trade. But this man is now being left out of President Trump's second term circle while Peter Navarro, the other trade adviser of the previous Trump presidency, incompetent and a loudmouth, is in. That does not bode well.

It was disconcerting when President Trump proposed a 10% tariff on Chinese imports some time ago, thus revealing a fundamental misunderstanding of trade dynamics. Such a tariff was going to be totally ineffective. It could not significantly impact the volume of Chinese goods entering the U.S., because meaningful effects of any tariffs can only begin at a 100% tariff or higher, given that Chinese production costs remain roughly half those of the US. For tariffs to be effective, they must level the playing field for American manufacturers—an obvious reality the White House has on ky recently understood. 245%! But will POTUS stay the course? He still has to assure us about that.

In this book, you will fins the whole background to what is wrong in our economic relation to China.

*****

Background

The increase in China's power happened with our money, and as this endangers the future of our democratic society, it puts all other considerations in the shadow. Considerations like "it is good for everyone to have cheap goods from China", even though this is a simple truth in itself, are being overshadowed by the danger to our future safety. Ending the flow of our money into China must be the overriding consideration, even if it will mean less of these cheap goods for all of us.

I get many reactions telling me it is too late already; China's power surge is unstoppable, they say. That may be so, but there is a catch here. That is, if we let this free trade continue, China will be sure to overwhelm us. That is a hard certainty. It is only if we stop this enrichment of China that is happening with our money, that we have a chance to see things turn out well in the end.

The point is, our Western society, with the US and the European Union as cornerstones, is different from other parts of the world. We are serious about freedom of speech, human rights, parliamentary control, an independent judiciary, the existence of unions, the right to strike, the right to demonstrate, etc., and we protect these values, while others protect them less or not at all. Dictators crush them. China is such a dictatorship and is, of course, afraid that our values will undermine its Communist power.

The real danger to our values and to our way of living, therefore, does not come from Moscow. Russian influence on the world stage has shrunk after the USSR collapsed in 1989. The February 2022 Russian invasion of Ukraine is an attempt by Mr. Putin to reverse that shrinking influence, but he should fail as we cannot afford to let this dictator win the Ukrainian war. After the many military and civilian deaths in this war, there now seems to be a stalemate there, so a truce will eventually have to be agreed upon, and then that's that. Russian influence will still be there, but it will be less than at the time of the USSR and, on condition that, up to the coming truce, we stay the course with providing weapons and other help to Ukraine, Putin's influence should not increase again. It seems President Trump is handling this well.

In sharp contrast, China's worldwide power and influence have increased with giant steps, year by year, since the year 2001. Unlike Moscow, it is Beijing that poses a real threat to the long-term survival of our free and democratic society.

To understand what is happening, we must first recognize our economic mistake of 2001. President Trump still has not done that. I thought that as long as we deny or ignore the original error we made and as we even continue making it year after year, we surely would not repair it.I thought one cannot repair a mistake one ignores! But POTUS is now doing just that, without explaining and recognizing the error! And it seems to work, but even now, the explaining is very necessary for the unrest to quieten down.

*****

This book, therefore, says four things.

1. Free trade with China was started in 2001 based on erroneous arguments and a total misreading of the inevitable consequences. That and climate change appear to be the two most important challenges we face. This book concentrates on the China problem.

2. Everybody now knows that, due to cheap competition from China, our industry is collapsing, especially the German industry, formerly the strength of Europe. The US will follow, and what we see now is only the beginning of this process.

3. Only the US can take the initiative to put things right here. President Trump is now doing that. But will he continue? To my deep shame and anger — as I am a European — Europe is incapable of action here. But still, if the US finally takes the initiative, the European Union will have to follow for the action to be a success. Ursula van der Leyen is still miles away from this vital understanding. That'll take time.

4. In order to silence the many loud voices purporting that "bringing trade with China back to manageable proportions has now become impossible", this book submits a scenario of one of the possible ways for the US to precisely do that and be successful. A way quite different, that is much better prepared,

8

than what the White House is doing now.

*****

PART ONE

Our major error with China and the secret fifth column

Chapter 1
Our major error.

Two things are infinite:

The universe and human stupidity.

Only about the universe, I am not quite sure.

Albert Einstein

China, almost unstoppably, is taking over world power.

Anyone who is unhappy with the growing power of China and the impossibility for our industry to compete with the low Chinese prices, needs to know the origin of the present shift in global equilibrium.

In the year 2000, President Clinton argued that we needed free trade with China. He made the US take that initiative, and the whole world followed his lead.

On March 8 of that year, speaking at the Paul Nitze School of Advanced International Studies in New York, a part of the Baltimore John Hopkins University, the President gave his arguments. The sheer absurdity of what he said there leaves no doubt that a single leader—and an entire nation with him—can be disastrously mistaken on a critical issue, putting the entire West at risk. Below, I quote the central portion of his speech, highlighting the six key errors the President made.

N365714 02: President Bill Clinton speaks at the Paul H. Nitze School of Advanced International Studies at Johns Hopkins University, in Baltimore, March 8, 2000. Clinton stressed the importance of having a permanent normal trade relationship with Ch (Photo by Mark Wilson) ·

This picture was taken on March 8, 2000, while President Clinton spoke the words cited here.

President Clinton, quote:

"The (coming) WTO agreement will move China in the right direction. It will advance the goals America has worked for in China for the past three decades. And of course, it will advance our own economic interests (1). Economically, this agreement is the equivalent of a one-way street (2). It requires China to open its markets—with a fifth of the world's population, potentially the biggest markets in the world—to both our products and services in unprecedented new ways. All we do is to agree to maintain the present access which China enjoys.

Chinese tariffs, from telecommunications products to automobiles to agriculture, will fall by half or more in just five years. For the first time, our companies will be able to sell and distribute products in China made by workers here in America, without being forced to relocate manufacturing to China (3), sell through the Chinese Government, or transfer valuable technology (4). For the first time, we'll be able to export products without exporting jobs (5). Meanwhile, we'll get valuable new safeguards against any surges of imports from China (6 !!!). "

unquote

I am not quoting President Clinton's incredible nonsense here to criticize him. Statesmen hardly ever have a macroeconomic education or understanding - with the famous exception of Deng Xiaoping, of course - and President Clinton was simply articulating what his economic and trade advisers had told him and what everyone seemed to have easily agreed upon at the time. More incredible than this enormous error by his advisors is that not a single professor of macro-economy at any of the many American universities even expressed doubt about this so patently wrong prediction, even though one couldn't ignore it, as it was cited in all newspapers. Hardly any skepticism came from Europe, either!

The consequence of this error and its present continuation is that China's power is growing greater than the US's and that this will eventually, step by step, spell the end of our manufacturing industry and following — inevitably — of our democratic free society.

13

The reason I am showing the Clinton nonsense at the beginning of this book is to make clear that, from time-to-time, unbelievable collective errors of thought and totally wrong insights on essential issues like this do really occur and that it is necessary to be skeptical and to verify what others think, every time a piece of information comes to us.

Still, this mistake by Clinton has never yet been acknowledged, let alone corrected. Admitting such an error is undoubtedly difficult, and politicians prefer to forget their missteps. Yet, similar grave mistakes are made repeatedly—even before our very eyes today. The real concern, however, is that Clinton's 2000 blunder has far more devastating consequences than all other mistakes that are regularly being made. This one continues to threaten the security of the Western world.

The WTO.

After the above speech, thanks to the US's towering international reputation in matters of economics, President Clinton's lead was followed world-wide, even by the WTO, the World Trade Organization. There, in Geneva, Switzerland, the supposed world-level professionals on trade showed total incompetence, even worse than what we saw by American macro-economic university professors, by ignoring, they too, what was evidently going to happen: Free trade with China was going to enrich Beijing beyond any previously known measure.

* * *

China's enrichment should have been predicted and stopped.

And predictable it certainly was! As China demanded to become member of the world trade organization WTO in 2001, it had three major differences from the other major players in world trade: the US, the European Union, fast-growing India, Brazil, Canada etc., etc.

First, China had, in the countryside, 400 to 600 million very low-paid but disciplined workers waiting for better times. No other country had, available and usable, so large a workers reserve, not even India. Second, China, with its Communist party apparatus, was and still is the only cruel and efficient dictatorship in this group of countries. Third, a few years before, Chinese leader Deng Xiaoping had changed the Chinese economy away from Marxism, where everything had belonged to the state and where competition had not existed, into functioning with our so much better system of ownership and competition. As a result, for the first time in China's history, it became organizationally possible to employ some of these 400 to 600 million low-paid workers in the country's production process.

Any university professor teaching Keynesian economics who knew his subject should have seen the danger coming and should have warned, but none did. None realized that this huge reservoir of cheap labor, combined with the dictatorship and the recent so much better internal market organization in China, would inevitably cause the trade imbalance we live with now.

*****

We had illusions.

At the time, in the West, we had a general feeling of superiority. In government circles, in our think tanks, in journalism, everywhere, we thought we were winning! As China had just joined our economic system, which is so much better than the Marxist system, we thought this was proof of our superiority. We were also convinced that after the USSR implosion in 1990, Communism in China would soon collapse too, and many predicted a collapse of the economy there as well. We now know all this did not happen, but these misguided illusions allowed our leaders to start free trade with China without even suspecting there might be a problem.

Beijing communism did not collapse, nor did its economy tank and they won't, but silly wishful thinking was everywhere in the US and other Western countries and can still be found now. There also was and still is this silly conviction that free trade is always good. Remember, too, that shortly after the year 2000, President Clinton visited Beijing and berated the Chinese as if they were stupid pupils. See, too, another speech by President Clinton, earlier in 1998, where he clearly was under the illusion that free trade would break down the Beijing dictatorship.[1]

Was Einstein right? Are we really infinitely stupid?

*****

How was it possible we were so terribly wrong?

Incorrect interpretation about something important occurs more often than we realize, generally because we fail to understand the inevitable underlying macro-economic process, especially so in circumstances never seen before. When things are new, as they were with China arriving on the market in totally new circumstances, we and that is almost everybody, allow our brains to stop functioning. Yes, when something is very new, we stop thinking!

For example, on the very subject of how to think about free trade, there has ever been only one good article. Only one! It is "The Folly of Free Trade ", published by economist John M. Culbertson in The Harvard Business Review, already in 1986. This brilliant insight — please read the first pages — was then completely ignored. [2] Unfortunately, the article was also terribly long-winded, which did turn away readers.

China is now becoming the most powerful country in the world economically and, following, politically and militarily. With our money, we are helping the exponential growth of our biggest opponent! Robert Lighthizer, in his book '*No Trade Is Free:*

---

[1] https://china.usc.edu/president-clintons-beijing-university-speech-1998
[2] https://hbr.org/1986/09/the-folly-of-free-trade`

Changing Course, Taking on China, and Helping America's Workers', wrote *"America is the first country in history to fund the rise of its rivals. We need to stop now, before it's too late."* (See further in Chapters 3 and 4). We would rather not say or write that we made this error; it is painful, and we continue to keep this under wraps. But silence here will inevitably lead to other wrong decisions. It must, therefore, be written:

Statement 1. In the year 2001, we entered into free trade with China on totally false assumptions.

This is the first of a few basic statements in this book. Some of these are an interpretation of facts, like the above one. Some others, like hereunder, consist of more generally abstract theorems that give an interpretation :

Statement 2. The real danger we face is not military. The dangerous rivalry for world power that is now being played out is economic.

To win this economic battle, we need good macro-economic understanding, but that is still absent, both in the US and, even in worse measure, in the European Union.

When looking back at what we keep doing wrong, must we conclude Einstein was right? Are we really infinitely stupid? This book tries to say "no!".

*****

So trade with China was initiated on wrong ideas. The resulting mess is now threatening the whole West. But only the White House can correct that. If not, the West will become the underdog to China and this process is now about halfway.

*****

In order to fully understand this book, it is necessary to realize that supposedly serious and competent people in high places still make the most incredible errors. For the reader who tends to be skeptical about this, please find here a little list of past and recent stupidities. It should be convincing.

1. The 2000 Clinton error, see Chapter 1.

2. The WTO trade experts blindly followed President Clinton's error.

3. Mr. Peter Navarro's error under President Trump, see page 34.

4. In Germany, in 1990, the decision to give the strong German currency to the new ex-soviet provinces of East Germany that had been under Marxist inefficiency for 45 long years, made almost everybody there redundant. The resulting misery was never recognized by the German government. This major economic error still rankles.

5. On June 27, 2022, leaders of the G7 countries (the United States, Canada, Germany, France, Italy, Japan, and the United Kingdom), at their G7 meeting in Elmau, Germany, wishing to counter the Chinese "Belt and Road" initiative, agreed on an infrastructure investment of 568 billion Euros to help our exports to China and elsewhere. This initiative ignored the root cause of the trade problem with China, which is that China can

produce at such a low cost. The G7 countries do not have enough products that can be exported to China and elsewhere, simply because we produce so much more expensively! A better transport infrastructure would do little to change this basic problem, and so these 568 billion Euros ($620 billion dollars) would be erroneously spent or, would better not be spent for this purpose at all. Even though the G7 came to their senses a bit later and the infrastructure was never made, this is another example of how our leaders can be blind to the most simple economic realities.

6. Until recently, the European Union had an Italian as its Commissioner For Economy, Mr. Paolo Gentiloni, who studied Political Science, not Economy and who has no economic knowledge whatsoever! He has been totally useless, for five years long. How can the Europeans be so idiotic?

7. In 2023, EU Commission President Ursula von der Leyen asked top financier Mario Draghi to submit a report on competition. Mr Draghi has no economic background either, and his report, published September 9, 2024, shows he doesn't. Mrs. von der Leyen should never have asked him.

8. And Mr. Draghi should never have accepted to write this report either. Although the report is excellent in its detailed enumeration and explanation of activities inside the EU where they can be more efficient, it fails to mention the one major economic problem that faces our competitiveness: China's low production costs. One must be an economic nitwit not to see that.

Draghi is.

9. In Brussels, that report is now being taken seriously, which is a major error in itself. Europe's economic agenda is now based on it!

10. On December 23, 2024, Newsweek published a wishful thinking prediction on China[3], and please note that this was written by the US-born son of a China-born father, now a US citizen! (See Chapter 7). This writer, Gordon Guthrie Chang, born July 5, 1951, is an American lawyer and political commentator known for his hawkish rhetoric on China.[1] He is the author of the 2001 book *The Coming Collapse of China,* in which he predicted the collapse of China by 2011. In December 2011, he changed the timing of the year of the predicted collapse to 2012. Did China collapse? It did not, but he again now writes the same total nonsense, and Newsweek published it!

This short selection of errors has a common element: a lack of macro-economic insight. One may even say, just look at Newsweek: a lack of common sense.

When we see those errors being made by our leaders and then being ignored or being taken seriously, and when we see there are so many of them, it becomes clear we must not believe too easily what we read. We must verify what we are being told, with our own common sense, always, always, always.

---

[3] https://www.msn.com/en-us/news/world/the-end-of-china-as-a-great-power-population-collapse-opinion/ar-AA1wnuBM

What lobbying will try to stop from happening.

To conclude this chapter, it should be understood that the opinion of this book, which is that we should convert this free trade into equal trade, will inevitably be severely countered by the business community. Powerful lobbying by industry to the United States government will push against the view in this book. That is because the business community can only look at the short term. Every CEO and every member of any board will deny what this book says, because, in the short term, they will fear it will affect their profitability. In our system, management gets appointed, judged and kept or fired by shareholders for its performance next quarter, this year and next year. The longer term, even if it is clear their industry may collapse, cannot interest them, the pressure for short-term results is too great.

This means the powerful business lobby will do all it can to make the government avoid what this book suggests.

This, in turn, has as a consequence that enacting what this book suggests will demand a high solidity of purpose at government level. The White House needs to see the longer-term interest of industry, an understanding the industry itself lacks! To succeed in this, our electorate will first have to be patiently and professionally informed, too.

*****

Chapter 2

How China Uses the Money It Earns From Its Exports.

To understand the influence of this free trade on the balance of world power, it is useful to look at what Beijing does with the money that flows into China.

First, it is not just the $3.4 trillion stockpile in Beijing's hands (see Chapter 4) that creates the current world imbalance, even though that stockpile is huge and we, in the West, have nothing to match it. More important is the fact that this stash is being replenished by an annual inflow of export to import excess money of roughly $600 billion, a huge amount as well. No other country has such an annual inflow. And this is still increasing. In 2022, it was $870 billion. A little dip may soon be seen, but growth will then resume. The export-to-import excess flow into China will likely reach one trillion per year soon.

A dual role.

First, this money supports the PRC's inherently ramshackle economy, which is vulnerable because it is run by the whims of the Communist Party and, for a large part, not by market rules. Had President Clinton not made his error, the economy of China would have continued to be and get into trouble, its growth impossible.

Stanford University published that, in early 2024, the invested capital of state-owned firms in China amounted to roughly 60% of total business capitalization.[4] The Communist party, all-powerful as it is, does not respect market rules. Both the party leadership in Beijing and individual provincial governments regularly decide on prestigious real estate investments that will not yield profits. With us in the West, investments are decided by those who also shoulder the businessman's risk. Not so in China. Many investments are initiated by high-level civil servants who have no idea of the market.[5] They give the order and then leave the financial consequence to others.

Empty Chinese real estate buildings with an eerie, abandoned atmosphere

This is the crux of why the Chinese economy is intrinsically weak and rickety. Non-yielding investments cost money. But there

---

[4] https://sccei.fsi.stanford.edu/china-briefs/reassessing-role-state-ownership-chinas-economy

[5] htt+ps://www.nytimes.com/2023/08/20/business/china-property-crisis-country-garden.html

is this huge stash of money, available to the Beijing government, increasing every year, that can easily compensate the real estate investment shortfalls. These shortfalls would create irreparable deficits and collapse the economy, where they not compensated by the free trade inflow. Thanks to this inflow, the Beijing government, whenever it sees fit, can fill those annual deficits with part of the 870 billion and thus keep the Chinese economy purring along. This removes a major economic headache for Beijing.

Second, a larger part of this annual 870 billion enables China to spend abroad, in Africa and elsewhere, with amounts — please forgive me for repeating it - that we, the Western democracies including the US, do not have available to us.

*****

How China mislead Sri Lanka

What China has done to Sri Lanka is a good example of how it uses this money now all over the world. Starting in 2010, Beijing bribed the country's then-corrupt government - yes, with money - so that it would accept a huge loan to build a new seaport. Then, contrary to unreliable due diligence provided by Beijing to the Sri Lankan government, the resulting income from that new seaport turned out to be much lower than predicted, not enough even to pay the low interest on the large loan. To cover that shortage, Beijing then offered a new loan, but at a much higher interest rate. This was accepted by the Sri Lankan government under Chinese threat of publication of their corruption. The result is that Sri Lanka is now completely stuck, unable to repay, and has had to cede large tracts of land to China as compensation. The corrupt government, having pocketed, then fell and was replaced by the opposition. Sri Lanka is now in big financial trouble. If China had not had its huge supply of money, coming from their free trade with us, this power grab by Beijing would not have been possible. In other words, the free trade agreement signed with China in the year 2001, based on the misconceptions as expressed by President Bill Clinton, enabled China's aggressive global power grab. Our "thinkers" are still not clear about that, but this is what has been going on for 23 years now.

Sri Lanka is now asking for help from us, the West.

In answer to that, on September 1, 2022, the IMF pledged a $2.9 billion loan to Sri Lanka Island on condition that it put its finances in order. In other words, Western money — the FMIs — is here helping redress the drama that China created with money coming from us in this free trade. In informing about this, our press, with only a very few fine exceptions, is grossly negligent. They separately report the parts, the loan, the pledge, and the lack of income, but rarely the complete picture that you read here.

With Pakistan, too, China behaved disgracefully. See the article: https://asia.nikkei.com/Spotlight/Belt-and-Road/385bn-of-China-s-Belt-and-Road-lending-kept-undisclosed-report?

The Communist regime in Beijing is not steering its country to be a good citizen of the world and is not bringing peace. It is willingly power-hungry and aggressive, as opposed to the US, that is actually quite benign.

*****

Chapter 3

The Trade Imbalance In Statistics And Figures.

And The Result

Dear reader, this chapter substantiates with figures and graphs what was written in chapters one and two. But if numbers and statistics are not your thing, just take the given facts for granted and skip this chapter.

*****

Since 2001, the trade imbalance between China and Western economies has grown significantly. We have been importing vast quantities of inexpensive Chinese goods, while China has accumulated the money we pay for them. At first glance, this may seem like a fair exchange—money for products—but there's a critical flaw. The average lifespan of these goods is just six years before they end up as waste, while the money we spend on them remains in China permanently. It is not a reasonable exchange at all. China, over these last years, has amassed this hitherto unprecedented amount of immediately usable money. Obtained from exporting, this money is usually called FER's or Foreign Exchange Reserves. The list hereunder, source the IMF, shows, for 31 countries, the accumulated Foreign Exchange Reserves over the last 21 years. You will see China's stash is now huge while Europe and the United States lack such a resource. We are already weak in comparison to China, but our newspapers, opinion writers anywhere, and our leaders keep silent about it. Our present weakness is not mentioned and, a fortiori, never with its cause: our wrong decision. Up till the present, no idea of redress at all has surfaced among the thinkers and advisers at the White House. It is high time for that to radically change.

Rank		Country or region	Foreign exchange reserves	Figures as of
		Foreign exchange reserves in millions of US Dollars		
1		China	3,305,419	May 2022
2		Japan	1,322,193	30-apr-22
3		Switzerland	1,033,369	30-apr-22
4		India	593,323	24 June 2022
5		Russia	582,3	17 June 2022
6		Taiwan	548,85	May 2022
7		Hong Kong	465,704	apr-22
8		Saudi Arabia	451,587	apr-22
9		South Korea	449,3	apr-22
10		Singapore	365,177	apr-22
11		Brazil	357,74	apr-22
12		Germany	277,782	apr-22
13		United States	241,975	27 May 2022
14		Thailand	242,43	apr-22
15		United Kingdom	231,293	apr-22
16		France	226,316	apr-22
17		Italy	211,419	apr-22
18		Mexico	209,567	22-apr-22
19		Israel	199,808	May 2022
20		Czech Republic	174,994	apr-22
21		Poland	142,252	January 2022
22		Indonesia	139,129	March 2022
23		United Arab Emirates	129,428	February 2022
24		Malaysia	115,762	February 2022
25		Turkey	107,66	6 May 2022
26		Philippines	106,757	apr-22
27		Canada	105,618	apr-22
28		Vietnam	102,872	July 2021
29		Spain	91,106	sep-21
30		Norway	88,058	aug-21
31		Iran	86	February 2020
-		European Union (ECB)	85,602	aug-21

Not very important in the above list but still interesting is:

Japan, relative to its population, has more reserves than China. But power is not about relative; it is about absolute numbers, and China, after only 21 years, already has three times as much as Japan. It took Tokyo 70 years to build up its reserves, and more importantly, Japan's reserves do not grow anymore as Japan's democracy has allowed the working class that produces the goods to steadily increase its income over the years. Japan is not so cheap anymore. In China, by brutal party dictatorship, the wages of workers in the manufacturing industry are kept very low.

Saudi Arabia's oil wealth has also been growing for much longer than seventeen years, but no matter how large it is relative to its population of only 33 million, in absolute terms, it is dwarfed by China's new wealth as well.

More important is that:

China's low costs remain low, and whoever claims they grow fast — and many authors do that — is giving the wrong information. China keeps its workers poor, even though the income of most of them has now risen just above the official poverty line. In 2020, a simple worker in China still costs only about 29% of what workers in the U.S. cost. Please realize what an enormous difference that is. That still makes it totally impossible for us to compete with Chinese products, and after 23 years with little change in those low costs, the resulting trade disequilibrium will continue over the next decades, unless we act.

See hereunder a bar chart of the hourly cost of labor, measured in U.S. dollars. Please look at China's costs, the $6.5 in 2020, on top of the light green column.

In July 2022, hourly wages in manufacturing in the US hovered around $25 an hour; in China, it was $7.2, the previously mentioned 29% of the US wage level. Cost in the EU is close to the US level. It is evident that we cannot compete with these Chinese prices. It should be evident, too, that with this price differential, the volume of exports from China is likely to increase, year after year, because China will increasingly be able to make technically more advanced products. Electric cars are such a new level of Chinese ability, a level they reached 5 years ago now.

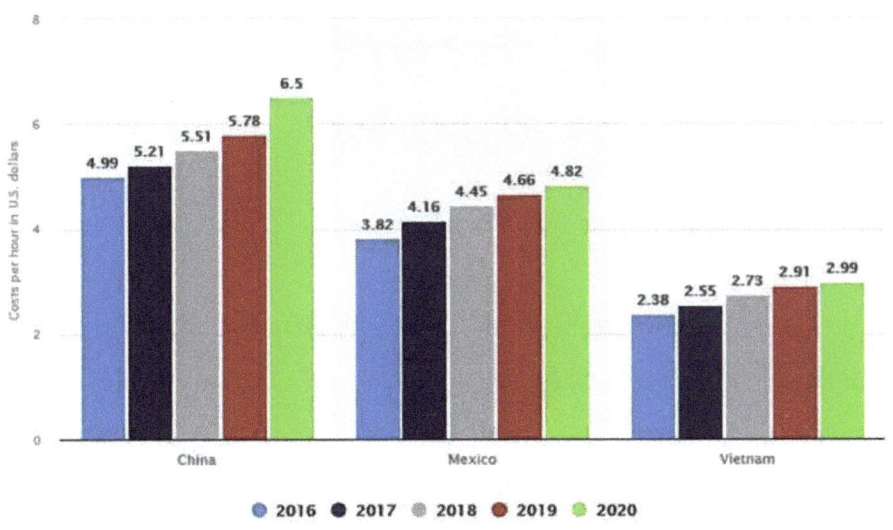

https://www.statista.com/statistics/744071/manufacturing-labor-costs-per-hour-china-vietnam-mexico/

And hereunder is a graph of China's immensely grown liquidity since 2001. Do keep in mind that this graph, at its bottom, starts at zero, that is, in 2000, China barely had any reserves. The increase of this stash each year is less than 600 billion because China spends a good portion of that yearly incoming 600 billion. In July 2022, it was US$3.1 trillion. (which is 3.1 with ten zeros.) China apparently wants to keep this available stash at around 3 trillion, as a reserve for future unforeseen economic problems.

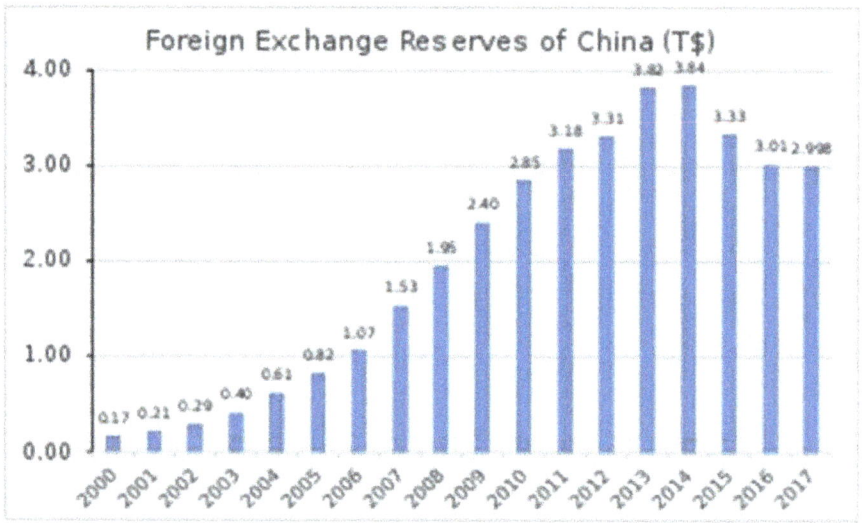

(The dip between 2014 and 2016 is mainly due to a large sale of dollars by Beijing in order to support China's then-weak currency.)

In all, China has amassed more than $10 trillion of FERs since 2001, of which it has already spent more than 7, some of it internally, most of it abroad. This more than 7 trillion spending explains the enormous Chinese acquisitions and loans we all know about in Africa and elsewhere in the world, of which the scandalous disaster inflicted by Beijing on Sri Lanka is but a small part.

China can spend more than, say, $400 billion every year without reducing its stock of 3 trillion! That is the core of the current Chinese danger. We are making China too rich and, therefore, too powerful.

Please note that the three trillion dollars still available to Beijing are liquid; that is, this large sum is available for spending whenever needed. The larger a country has such a fortune in easily spendable form, the more it has economic power abroad.

A widespread misunderstanding must, therefore, be corrected:

Statement 3. The economic power exercised abroad by any nation does not depend on the size of its gross domestic product (GDP), as is still generally assumed by economists all over the world. It is, in fact, determined by the size of its available liquid assets, i.e., by how much money it can easily spend abroad each year.

*****

Consequences of the present situation.

- China, already now, has a greater influence in Africa than we have, thanks to their generosity with money.
- Corrupting governments, China lends to poor countries who then cannot pay back the loan and thus fall in its power.
- China is buying — with money again — political influence within the European Union:

> ➤ through Greece, after having poured money into upgrading its harbour of Piraeus
> ➤ in the so-called 16 + 1 [6]
> ➤ through Hungary.

This is totally unacceptable.

The above may not interest the US, but it shows how insidious China is behaving in the balance of world power. Although by now, the intrusive political Chinese influence inside the EU is running out of public credibility and sympathy, which is a good thing, the whole action, as China tried to wield influence and disruption within the EU, is another example of China trying to sneakily gain power everywhere in the world, and is doing so with money, that is, the free trade money coming from us.

Another consequence of the production cost difference is that major Western industries are now relocating their production to China, simply to stay in business. If this trend continues, it will mark the beginning of the end for Western manufacturing. Consider the following example:

In May 2024, the German chemical giant BASF decided to relocate a large part of its German production facilities to China, simply to remain able to make a sound profit in the short and medium term. The Chinese regime, of course, receives them in a

---

[6] The '16 + 1' :
https://en.wikipedia.org/wiki/Cooperation_between_Chin
a_and_Central_and_Eastern_Eu

most friendly way, but this means that BASF brings 40% of their production assets under the might and whim of this dictatorship. BASF's money and profit will be made for a large part in China, not much in Germany anymore.

For this, BASF cannot be blamed, they do what is needed to survive. It is a decision by the government that created free trade, with this horrible process as a result. The industry itself cannot change these conditions. The error was made by the government, so it is for the government to repair.

And again, our "thinkers", with only very few exceptions, do not see what is going on. They do not wish to see it!

One of those few exceptions to this is, in the Netherlands, a locally well-known thinker and writer, who has founded his own think tank, 'HCCS', in the city of The Hague. This Leiden University Professor, Rob de Wijk, in a recent book, put it clearly: *" (As against China) the Western world order with its free-market economy, international law, international institutions, democracy, human rights, and civil liberties is going down the drain. How to turn this tide is becoming the most important question of our time."*[7] Professor de Wijk is still relatively unknown outside the Netherlands, but compared to other thinkers and writers in the EU

---

[7] https://www.bruna.nl/boeken/de-nieuwe-wereldorde-9789463822121?utm_source=adtraction&utm_medium=affiliate&utm_campaign=adtraction&at_gd=04A07649096BFB4209658457AE70DDA49F5E8202

and the US, this man is brilliant. His only weakness is that he changes the subject of his attention the whole time.

The obvious next question then is *'how to turn this tide'*. Finding an answer to that requires macro-economic knowledge, and what is more, it requires insight into how to apply this Keynesian knowledge in practice. Chapter 4 tries to give an answer.

More consequences of this free trade

Another positive exception was, already five years ago, on August 26, 2017, what Jason Horowitz and Liz Alderman wrote in the New York Times:

quote

"While Europe was busy squeezing out Greece, the Chinese dove in with bucketloads of investments that are beginning to pay off, not only economically, but also through the political influence China gained within the European Union.[8]

Last summer, Greece prevented the European Union from issuing a joint statement against Chinese aggression in the South China Sea. In June, Athens, using the veto power the EU member countries have, also prevented the EU from condemning China's human rights record. Days later, it opposed stricter screening of Chinese investments in Europe. Hungary, where China has pledged

---

[8] see also in Chapter 9, the section on Wolfgang Schäuble, the now defunct German Minister of Finance.

to spend billions on a railroad, is the other country that has blocked the EU's declaration on the South China Sea."

unquote

Money earned in the existing free trade, was here used to bribe the Greeks and the Hungarians. This empowers Beijing.

*****

Our reaction to all this

In 2016, President Trump, before his inauguration, had already denounced our Chinese trade relation, saying "jobs have been taken away". This is the other result of the trade imbalance. In fact, the loss of jobs was not so bad, but the enrichment is. Later, after he had become President, Mr. Trump instructed his adviser for trade, Mr. Peter Navarro, to stop the huge influx of Chinese products. Mr. Navarro's then put tariffs on Chinese goods in what came to be known as 'the tariff war'. But Mr. Navarro did not understand that, when one adds import tariffs to the cost of the Chinese products coming into the US market, these goods may still be a bit cheaper than the same product that could be manufactured in the US. That is what happened with his tariffs, and people just kept buying Chinese! This was, of course, foreseeable, but not for Mr. Navarro. He never either corrected his error, nor did our vaunted press ever put its finger on the incredible incompetence of this man. Navarro failed dismally. At the end of his tariff war, which lasted two years, China's trade surplus with the US had not been halved, had not even been reduced; it had increased by one percentage point! As incompetent as this man, so excellent was his colleague Robert Lighthizer. But Mr. Lighthizer had not been given the authority Mr. Navarro had.

Recently, even with President Biden's capable advisers, such as Kurt Campbell, the issue of China's growing economic dominance has been poorly addressed. Instead of a comprehensive strategy, the response has been fragmented—like the 100% tariff on electric cars, which is merely a small bandage on a deep, festering wound. These 100% tariffs surely protect the American car industry, but they fail to address the basic danger of China's enrichment. Right now, our trade relationship with China is still not being correctly repaired. We have a wait and see what President Trump will do now in his second presidency.

Meanwhile, China is cautious

Beijing does not want to alarm our public opinion and, therefore, remains discreet about its growing power. It quietly wishes its trade advantage to last as long as possible into the future. Negative public opinion might cause us to buy less, so clever Beijing keeps very quiet.

...and has a real talent for Public Relations

An example of this talent was shown already twenty years ago when, as a last demand before allowing Chinese membership, the WTO wanted China to let its currency float freely. A reasonable demand. China's eventual enrichment would thus be accompanied, as would have been appropriate, by a steady rise in the value of the Renminbi, and this would have tended to reestablish the previous worldwide equilibrium. To counter this demand, the Chinese government mounted a truly brilliant Public Relations campaign, for which the then-German Chancellor Schröder, an opportunist in the bad sense of the word, was the first to capitulate. Mr. Schröder hoped to come on friendly terms with the 'new' Beijing and sell more Mercedes' and BMWs to China. He said floating the currency was unnecessary. Jacques Chirac, then French president, a good legal thinker but notorious for a total lack of economic understanding, didn't want to be left behind. He let it be known that Paris, too, did not think floating the Chinese currency was necessary. This left the US, with the UK under Blair on a leash, as the only powerful voices in the WTO to demand the floating of the currency. Beijing's subtle Public Relations machine then began to portray Washington as a jealous regime that did not grant reborn China its place under the sun. In the US, George W. Bush had just been inaugurated, had to respond to 9/11, and wanted to launch his catastrophic pre-emptive war against Iraq. He found the Chinese talk annoying, and — under this very clever Chinese pressure — he too gave in. Blair followed obediently.

This episode shows how cleverly the Chinese can play our Western opinion, our journalists, our thinkers, and our governments and get away with it.

It is only over the last four years that our public opinion about China has begun to be more negative. It was high time.

Another example of Chinese subtlety is to be found in Xi

Jinping's speech in Davos on 17 January 2017, now eight years ago. In a friendly, generous tone, Mr Xi expressed the importance of free global trade for all. This was picked up by our newspapers as an important message as opposed to what President Trump had said. But to my frustration, not one opinion article made mention of the fact that this speech was simply an 'oratio pro domo', given that it clearly implied a continuation of the existing trade advantage for China. Again here, our press understood and informed beside the point. Even the Washington Post, which in my eyes has the best-thinking editors in the world, did not see this speech for what it was. Neither did the formerly so insightful French newspaper "Le Monde" give a correct comment on this Xi speech. We are incredibly short-sighted.

Anti-Chinese?

I am sometimes asked if I am anti-Chinese. Truth is, I like the Chinese very much. I have had a daughter company in Beijing, have been there 25 times to manage it, have been married to a fine and very beautiful Chinese woman, and have two wonderful children with her. The Chinese are an admirable people. As I had, since 1993, this wonderful Chinese in-law family, in which almost all were members of the Communist party, I knew about the hard determination of this radical and cruel regime. I knew democracy would not come to China.

While I like the Chinese people and admire them, I do have a problem with this aggressive communist dictatorship. The war in

Ukraine, for now, diverts attention from the danger of China's growth, but the Chinese danger is greater.

The Power of China

Recently, in our press, there was triumphant cheering when Chinese growth stagnated (summer 2022), but the trade surplus did not shrink much. A bit later, it started growing again, and its size, even if it were again to shrink a little in the future, will continue to be there. Huge enrichment, even if temporarily just a few percentage points less, continues to be huge enrichment. And China's research is now overtaking us. [9]

Healthy skepticism

In our daily lives, we do not yet feel the financial power that China already wields. Many people, therefore, have a healthy skepticism about this power. Is this not being exaggerated? That is a legitimate question. So, allow me to put things in perspective with two examples.

I. We all know that China was building a 'New Silk Road', the BRI, or the Belt and Road Initiative. They are doing this to make it easier for their goods to be shipped to the West. One key component of the BRI is a planned railway line through Pakistan, with an estimated cost of $57 billion USD. This large sum is still only 2% of the current Chinese foreign exchange reserves you read about hereabove. So, it is easy for China to advance money for this

---

[9] Finfacts Ireland: China world leader in 37 of 44 critical technologies, EU missing

railway. But if the US wanted to do anything of similar magnitude, either our small foreign exchange reserves would be halved, which would probably be unacceptable to Congress, or we would have to raise our debt ceiling by that amount.

II. As early as in 2017, on May 17, the New York Times wrote about the BRI:

quote

"...The initiative, called "One Belt, One Road," looms with a scope and scale with little precedent in modern history, proposes more than $1 trillion in infrastructure and stretches across more than 60 countries."

end quote

$1 trillion is now completely beyond anything the US or the EU can do. But it is still only a third of what China has in its coffers.

China is building this new Silk Road for its export. Beijing wants the disbalance of trade and the lovely source of money from the West to continue.

These two examples will hopefully dispel any doubt as to how great China's money power is.

*****

China accuses us.

China accuses the US of aggression in return, but there is a difference there. China wants to take Taiwan, which has a democratic regime, different from their dictatorship. We should compare that with the US attitude towards Cuba, an island near our coasts with, like Taiwan to China, a different regime to ours. Cuba is Communist. In 1962, Havana tried to place Russian ballistic nuclear missiles on its territory. President Kennedy prevented that, but after that, did the US ever want to take Cuba? Of course not. The White House has always wished us to be a peaceful country respectful of others. Sure, the CIA has made huge errors against this principle in the past. But has Taiwan ever tried, like Cuba, to aim aggressive attack weapons at its neighbor China? Absolutely not, but China wants to take Taiwan, while we do not wish to take Cuba. This is just one example of the fundamental difference between the two aggressivities of the US and China.

Another item of Chinese aggression is shown in their tampering with worldwide rules on territorial waters that have existed since the 17th century. The Dutch scholar Hugo Grotius (1583 – 1645) wrote about "Mare Liberum", the freedom of the sea. After that, worldwide agreements on territorial waters began to take shape. The 12-mile limit was formally adopted as an international standard in 1958 with the Geneva Convention on the Territorial Sea and the Contiguous Zone. Currently, the United Nations Convention on the Law of the Sea supports this rule, and it has been ratified by more than 150 nations. But in 1947, China declared the so-called South China Sea to be its territorial waters and did not sign, although that sea stretches more than 1300 nautical miles from its coast! The surface of this sea is 1.35 million mi^2, larger than the Caribbean with its 1.06 million square miles. Has the US ever considered calling the Caribbean its own? Of course not. More recently, the PRC has established bases on previously uninhabited atolls in the China Sea. That is another element of the difference. The PRC is aggressive, the US is not.

Also, President Trump suddenly naming the Gulf of Mexico Gulf of America still does not mean a military grab like China's military grab in the South China Sea.

Chapter 4

The only possible solution

This Chapter gives the second basic message of this book, which is still being disputed almost everywhere: It says the only way to prevent China from becoming the most powerful country in the world is by stopping free trade with it.

Allow me once more to cite the Dutch Professor Rob de Wijk, the founder of the think tank HCCS in The Hague, about China's increasing power: *"The Western world order with its free-market economy, international law, international institutions, democracy, human rights, and civil liberties is going to end. The great question to answer is: What can we do about it?"*. Professor de Wijk sees it right, but he has no answer to his question. This book provides one.

Putting tariffs on some or all Chinese products will not stop China's enrichment, nor is the too-radical view of 'decoupling' of any use. Only the replacement of the present free trade with Equal Trade will do the job. By Equal Trade, it is meant here that "measured in value, there may not be more imports from China to the US than exports from the US to China". Let such equal trade be in as great a volume as desired, and let us forget the too-primitive idea of decoupling.

If ending free trade with China is the only way forward, the next question, of course, is: "How?".

When talking about this, supposedly wise people who, in fact, are not wise at all, will immediately react in chorus: "It is too late; we cannot stop this free trade anymore". Fortunately, once more, that opinion is incorrect; like all the previous nonsense that has been written about democracy coming to China, the Chinese prices moving up quickly, Mr. Xi Jinping to lose power soon, or the Chinese economy soon tanking. It certainly will be difficult to end free trade with China, and at the US government level, it will require very high skill and subtlety in trade and business affairs, with a strong hand. But possible it certainly is.

In order to answer the many voices that still say "impossible", this chapter outlines a clear scenario, a how-to-do-it, and in theory, this is simple. It consists in repairing the 2001 mistake made by President Clinton and undoing the consequences of the WTO's shortsightedness. It means reducing the flow of money from our economies into China that allows China to prop up its rickety economy and get so very rich and powerful, so quickly.

But to implement this reversal of the wrong decision will be complicated and very difficult. And mindsets will have to change. Talk of ending free trade is still taboo, but the beginning of a turnaround in public opinion and in the press, a first condition for success, is beginning to dawn.

If regulating trade with China succeeds, what will that do?

If the US, in cooperation with the EU, limits free trade with China, China will still have its stock of 3 trillion FER dollars. But the influx of over 600 billion every year would dry up. China can then hold out for a few more years until its continued spending will have reduced its 3 trillion stash to roughly 1 trillion. Past experience shows that Beijing will not want to reduce that further, but will keep such reserve for a rainy day, and therefore will predictably stop spending. It is only then — that is, about two years later — that the real fragility of the Chinese economy will kick in. Will Beijing then be able to stop making the wrong investments that are her economic Achilles Heel? Well, that is unlikely, because one doesn't change the economic habits of a huge dictatorship with so many civil servants overnight, nor in three years either. That will likely take much longer and it will be beneficial to us. In other words, ending free trade will only get its beneficial effect a few years after it has been done, but then it will really produce the desired effect. The essential activity is to hugely reduce the enrichment of China's economy. Does the US have the patience for that, and will the EU go along? I have serious doubts, but nevertheless, stopping this free trade is the only solution that can protect us from onrushing China's becoming our boss in the long term.

*****

GENERALLY ACCEPTED OPINION IN THE US.

General opinion on China, has yet to take a turn.

In stopping free trade with China, huge business interests are involved, everyone can see that. In planning to replace free trade with equal trade — that is, measured in money, back-and-forth trade with China is to become of roughly equal amounts, every year — all

47

the companies that now buy in China and distribute here - this is how many make their money at present - will fiercely oppose reducing free trade. The lobbying by industry to stop the government from ending free trade will predictably be ferocious, even if it will be short-lived. The White House should be well prepared to face such an onslaught in order to stay the course.

A lot will have to change.

As yet, the idea of stopping free trade is not being discussed anywhere, not in the opinion press, not in average journalism, nor in the best think tanks on either side of the Atlantic, not even, as far as I know, indoors in Washington. People do speak of 'decoupling', but decoupling is a silly 'black-and-white' idea. For now, with only a few exceptions, the message of this book stands alone. But at the same time, in general opinion, the need to stop the money flow to China begins to dawn. People say the Chinese have a long-term view. We need ours.

What else is hindering?

Radically altering ongoing trade relations between two countries or groups of countries to be enacted by government has never been done before. Something so new and so drastic will arouse great opposition, but it consists of nothing other than a late but proper response to that other novelty, the huge "Reservoir" of cheap labor in China, and the subsequent enrichment by us of our adversary. New things often meet resistance, and no doubt this solution will find resistance too. Our leaders, in the US and in Europe, will have to prepare themselves and their public opinion for this new measure.

I nevertheless fear that when finally the need to stop the flow of money into China will be understood and accepted - which I am persuaded will eventually happen - it will come too late.

Albert Einstein was probably right; we are incredibly stupid.

*****

Here then, notwithstanding my skepticism, is an example, a scenario of how, with the US in the lead, changing the free trade flow from China into 'Equal Trade' can be done. I have published this scenario earlier, in a slightly different form, in a few articles in the Dutch weekly called 'EW magazine'[10] and in my Dutch book. But it is in the US that this message needs to be read.

*****

The how.

If the US wanted to take a first step and gradually end free trade with China in a very simple way, the White House could start by deciding that, from a fixed date, no electric cars from China would be allowed to be imported anymore. This would be a strong measure, and it would set the tone for what would follow. But this would still be a primitive, partial action towards the problem. It would be seen

---

10

https://www.ewmagazine.co.uk/opinion/background/2021/03/ hoe-joe-biden-china-nog-kan-stoppen-807707/

as an action to protect US car makers, but it would not be understood as a first step in halting our enrichment of China.

There are more complete actions possible where, in enacting them, everybody will understand what the White House is doing.

*****

Scenario

This is just one of the several ways it could be done.

So here it is.

In a major speech, the President apologizes publicly for the mistake that, in 2001, led the US to sign a free trade agreement with cheap-producing China, explains in a few sentences why that disrupts the world equilibrium, announces the US's intention to bring trade on a more normal footing and on the same day, politely informs China about this decision as well.

Legally, since this would alter the terms the U.S. agreed to in 2001 at the WTO, a formal notice should be sent to Geneva, informing the organization that the U.S. is terminating the agreement. This move should be accompanied by the explanation that it is an effort to create a more balanced and fair global trade system.

On the same date, but after careful previous preparation, the White House announces which sectors of our own industry will be banned from buying from China after a six-month transition period, starting from that very date as well. Should banned goods from

China arrive at US air and seaports after that six-month period, they will not be unloaded. POTUS states that the present open free trade will be replaced by '*Equal Trade*', i.e., the United States will be happy to allow China to export to the United States, but measured in money roughly in equal quantities of what the US exports to China, not more. The more trade the better, as long as it will be roughly equal. Next, in this speech, the industrial sectors that will still be allowed to buy from China will clearly be indicated and those that may not anymore buy there too. The sectors that may continue to buy from China will be chosen so as not to become strategically dependent on it.

To take a simple example, imports of clothing, t-shirts, jeans, and the like would be allowed to continue. But many other industries, including, of course the military industry, will have to make 100 % of their purchases in the United States. What will have to be regulated in detail is that some of the other industries that are no longer allowed to import from China will also no longer be allowed to import from other cheap outside countries such as Vietnam, Indonesia, and India, at least not suddenly in larger volumes than they do so far. That, too, will have to be clearly regulated. Complicated it will be, but entirely possible.

To get all this right, the United States will already have set up a new Im- and Export Trade Bureau. This new government agency will be tasked with setting the rules, organizing control, noting what goes wrong, and adjusting the rules where necessary. The White

House will appoint a capable official to head this trade bureau. This official will certainly have a difficult task that will cost him and his staff a lot of work.

The equally gigantic but short-lived lobbying efforts that the US business community will predictably come up with to block such a presidential initiative should be strictly regulated so that the new bureau will be able to do its job relatively undisturbed. From day one, all companies in the sectors that have only six months left before they are banned from importing from China will know that they will have to move their sourcing to other countries as soon as possible, partly other low-cost foreign countries, such as Vietnam, Indonesia, and India, but for the most part back to the US itself. Per the industrial sector, these quantities will be regulated. A delaying factor will be that some firms will have to invest quickly in new production capacity outside China, mostly in the United States itself. After all, the goods that are no longer coming from China will have to be made elsewhere. Therefore, for some industrial sectors, the said six-month period may turn out to be too short and will have to be extended. Let it remain clear, importing in itself is not very harmful. It is the enrichment of China that is harmful and must stop. So it is the import from China that has to be curtailed. When the industry will thus be forced by clear government rules to relocate its sourcing, it will undoubtedly respond with a very high efficiency. After all, survivalism is at the core of business' DNA.

President Joe Biden had already vaguely announced his

intention in the above sense but still remained unclear on the overall goal. At present, Washington's thinking is still about protecting our own industry. that thinking still needs to be changed into the goal of stopping China's enrichment. Protecting our industry will be an automatic result, but it should not be the overall goal as it is now, with the reigning short-sightedness.

What the above boils down to is the government will finally fix what it has done wrong.

*****

Three counterarguments refuted

Whoever talks about cancelling free trade with China is immediately confronted with what Dutch China expert Henk Schulte Nordholt wrote, in a reaction to my writing, on August 21, 2020, in *EW-magazine: "Prisse does not take into account the complex global trade and investment flows of which China is now inseparable."*

However, this claim is simply incorrect. These trade flows are not inherently inseparable from China, nor is China from them. The argument suggests that after 23 years of economic entanglement, unraveling these ties is impossible—but that is far from the truth.

In reality, a company's decision to source parts or raw materials from China can be adjusted within months. Likewise, shifting to suppliers in another country—or back to the United States—would take only slightly longer. Businesses, driven by the instinct to survive, adapt rapidly when necessary. If the government mandates a change, companies will restructure their supply chains with remarkable speed.

As written here before, there surely will be fanatical lobbying to counter this scenario, because the business world can only think in the short term. That is the consequence of our system where for management, the next quarter's report is very important, because a sudden lowering of the share price of the company would open the possibility of an unwanted takeover. Therefore, immense pressure on the immediate short-term comes from shareholders and other stakeholders. The business world cannot think for the long term, except for the special areas of research, production capacity, and choosing "what do we want to be our products?". Managers always proudly deny they are being forced into this fundamental short-term view, but it is the simple truth. The pressure they live under for the short term is immense. It is, therefore, up to the government to look after the longer-term interest of business. The government has a better perspective and understanding of the future than the business community itself is capable of.

But that expected lobbying will say one thing right: inevitably, stopping free trade with China will bring a brief recession. The lobbyists will say that correctly, but that small recession will predictably be short, and it will also predictably turn into a fierce economic success. In other words, the cause of a recession will be short-lived, and so will the small recession itself.

Difficult, then, for sure. And there will be a short-lived chaos, too. The motivation to do all this anyway should be that we must, at all costs, avoid Chinese world domination. We have to choose: do we want to protect our democratic society from oncoming China, or is Nout Wellink, ex-President of the Dutch National Bank, who has extensively worked for Chinese banks, right in saying that the US will soon "dangle behind China"?[11] That choice is actually not difficult at all. There is no middle ground. It's the one or the other. Either we stop free trade with China, or we do not, period.

A second objection that can be dismissed here is: 'But then everything will become more expensive, that is unacceptable!' It isn't however, because it need not be at the expense of our quality of life and, what is even more important, this will hardly have any economic consequences. After the gradual cessation of large-scale purchases in China, the amount of money subsequently spent by consumers in the United States is expected to remain roughly the same; only the volume of goods bought with this money will decrease, because those goods will have become more expensive, like they were before 2000, in our healthy economy at the time. According to Keynes (1883-1946), the British economist who was the first to correctly explain how a country's economics works, only the amount of money spent is important for the health of the

---

[11] Mr. Welling was President of the Dutch National Bank, (The Dutch 'Fed') from 1997 to 2011. He then started to work for the largest Chinese banks and became fully convinced China would become more powerful than te US and would soon dominate the world.

economy, not what is bought for it. So the 'everything is getting more expensive' is correct, but a little less luxury for consumers as a price for stopping Chinese supremacy in our lives, is not a difficult choice. And again, 'more expensive' does not hurt the economy.

Of course, governments will have to explain in advance to the general public why this sacrifice is necessary. Already, Robert E. Lighthizer, one of President Trump's former trade representatives, not an economist but a diplomat and excellent thinker, explained this in an article in *The New York Times* in May 2000 and later in his book. In this article, Lighthizer nicely navigated between the nonsense of his boss, Trump, whom he did not want to contradict, and reality, which he succeeded in pointing out without shocking his master.

Source:

https://www.nytimes.com/2020/05/11/opinion/coronavirus-jobs-offshoring.html

More important, the brilliant Mr. Lighthizer is the only serious author in the US who, in his book "Free Trade with China Has to Stop," gives the same opinion about free trade as I do, although his idea is based on the wish to protect American jobs. That argument is weak because the US has almost full employment. I argue China is getting too rich and will dominate the world, and I say that it must stop. Mr. Lighthizer and I have two very different arguments, but we come to the same conclusion. This free trade must be converted into a trade that eliminates the disequilibrium.

Mr. Lighthizer also writes, "America is the first country in history to fund the rise of its rivals."[12]. He says it right.

In this year 2025, he most certainly would have liked to put his thoughts into action, but President Trump has not chosen him. We can only hope that will change.

The third argument, that China is not dangerous because it has insurmountable problems, is well articulated in Dinny McMahon's 2018 book: *China's Great Wall of Debt*. Mr. McMahon writes what he believes are four reasons that will automatically kill the Chinese economy: a) the far too great ease with which loans are granted for all kinds of projects that can never be repaid, b) the enormous corruption and its negative impact on the economy, c) the amount of new construction in suburbs of many cities that are not being lived in and, finally, d) the disproportionate ageing of the population in the face of too few children due to China's long-standing one-child policy. These four arguments are all true, but we have been hearing almost all these since 2003 and yet things are still not going wrong in China. So, how is that possible?

Well, that nothing goes wrong, while the four arguments are correct, is due both to the huge $870 billion a year that helps China

---

[12] https://www.amazon.com/No-Trade-Free-Changing-Americas/dp/0063282135/ref=sr_1_fkmr0_1?crid=3UN0L4TAEP18Z&dib=eyJ2IjoiMSJ9.lbaHR-78jxUe_gg66cvhUMSU__K4xGsj4Bd7dcz53LQ_OH_Vhz1-hGRMci0JcuWs.GaynsgXeIPgEmlZdQ_D2uMpr7aza0CYIsRfnOqIxZ4I&dib_tag=se&keywords=Robert+E.+Lighthizer&qid=1725391838&sprefix=robert+e.+lighthizer%2Caps%2C262&sr=8-1-fkmr0

economically keep its head above water, and also to the existence of still roughly 300 million very poor, ready-to-work Chinese in the countryside and finally to the might and cruelty of the Beijing Communist dictatorship that keeps workers' salaries low. So let there be no doubt: despite China's major internal challenges, its economy will stand up as long as the skewed free trade continues. What McMahon's book, on the other hand helps us understand is that the Chinese economy could collapse like a house of cards if the US managed to end free trade. Only then would the Chinese regime face the consequences of its dishonesty, its cruel treatment of its citizens, and its relentless pursuit of power—traits of oppression and deception that we must ensure never take root here.

I also wish to cite and give a comment here on writing by a Dutchman, Mr. Henk Schulte Nordholt, because this man, who is seen as a China expert in the Netherlands, shares both the errors and the qualities of the average American writer. In the Dutch weekly *EW magazine,* he submitted an article called 'Until China changes'. Already with this title, he let his wishful thinking run wild. After all, China is changing in precisely the opposite direction of his prediction that it will become milder. China is becoming more aggressive and more cruel by the year, not milder. Second, he calls on the democratic nations, in joint action, to hold China 'to the rules'. This sounds nice, but even if this were to make China strictly play by all the WTO trade rules, the trade imbalance enrichment would not stop. It is also an illusion to think that all democratic countries would cooperate in holding China to rules. Beijing's 'divide-and-conquer-with-money' has proved too effective to hope for that. Consider, for instance, China's successful anti-EU political influence in Greece.

While these first two not very correct ideas undermine the whole article, Schulte Nordholt does see some things very clearly: the Chinese threat does indeed concern all democratic countries in the world, and he also sees that "the doom of the Occident is in sight" and: "international trade strengthens the main pillar on which the legitimacy of the Communist Party of China rests: economic growth". So he mentions trade, but does not see its negative effect. But then again, he rightly writes: *"(Xi cherishes) the dream that the Chinese elite has been obsessing over since the disastrous Opium War of 1840: he wishes to see the country return to the number 1 position to which it is naturally entitled because of its size and superior civilization. If the CPC succeeds, the end of the Westphalian order of equality between states is in sight. Equality never existed (with the Chinese)."* And *"Because the US is the only power that can still stop China, democratic countries should raise that politically with the US"*. Schulte Nordholt clearly sees the danger and he also correctly articulates the US position. He is just not able to imagine a remedy. This would require macroeconomic insight, a discipline Mr Schulte Nordholt is not familiar with.

The 55, 25, and 20% - ratio

For that remedy now, the West depends on the US for the

initiative and Europe for following. Indeed, only the United States can still stop China, and then only if they get it right. President Trump will soon have a unique, and perhaps the last chance to do so. This President certainly has the guts, which is wonderful, but he is also likely to choose incompetent advisers again.

Another reason why the EU cannot take that initiative is because it only accounts for about 25% of China's huge annual trade surplus. With the United States, China's trade surplus is roughly twice that! The last 20% consists of the money from purchases in China from the rest of the world. If the EU alone were to curtail or end free trade with China, Beijing would simply be irritated. But if the United States, which till recently accounted for 55% of China's surplus, were to stop that trade, the Chinese economy would really be hurt.

Note that the 55-25-20 ratio is a rough index. Each year, it fluctuates slightly, and right now, the 55% for the US is now reducing, but basically the relation remains roughly the same year after year.

'Difficult' is no excuse for doing nothing, but whether it will happen, I doubt.

A German misconception

Another example of naivety is the German government's misunderstanding of her self-interest. There is a firmly entrenched fallacy in thinking there. Germany is the only country of the Western democracies to have had, until recently, a trade surplus with China. In 2022, they had a $77-billion-euro export to China against a $66-

billion euro import. It is, of course, very impressive that the Germans manage this, despite the cost of production in China being so low. They do this thanks to their technical superiority and their wonderful work ethic. Thus, the Germans feel comfortable; they consider themselves strong and do not see, or do not want to see, that China's gigantic annual enrichment of about $870 billion poses a threat to Germany too, just as much as to all other democracies. $870 billion is really more — and gives more power — than that nice little $11 billion. And yet, in the eyes of the Scholz government, with that very strong industrial lobby he has to contend with, they still see the protection of German business interests in China as of greater importance than the danger Chinese global power poses. They are short-sighted. Will the next Chancellor, Mr. Merz, see more clearly? That is still uncertain.

This fallacy is also described by Belgian China expert Professor Jonathan Holslag, as he wrote in a recent article. In late 2000, the German government managed to convince Brussels to sign a trade agreement with China. Chancellor Angela Merkel wanted to push this through absolutely, and because of this limited German thinking, China seemed to succeed in driving an initial wedge between the EU and President Joe Biden's United States. In the game of divide and conquer, the Chinese were once again masters, and Brussels allowed itself to be placated. Fortunately, there was much opposition to this agreement, and in the end, the European Parliament refused to ratify this agreement. Thankfully, we in

Europe are not stupid all the time!

Dictatorial capitalism

Thanks to its dictatorial power, its culture of cracking down, imposing rules and rock-hard discipline, China seemed to have mastered the coronavirus. Nevertheless, the growth rate of China's economy went down temporarily to +3.9%, according to the IMF; and a contraction might even follow later. But here again, our silly press was cheering too early. Even in the event of a contraction, China's trade surplus will remain huge, and the enrichment will continue. Even if that surplus were to decrease by a gigantic 5%, the remaining 95% would simply continue the dangerous enrichment. It won't go to zero; it'll stay huge.

The main objective of this book is that correct insight eventually reaches the US political leadership. In both the United States and Europe, a majority of the press and population still think that free trade everywhere, including with China, is a good thing. As long as the White House continues to sanction the Clinton mistake that we then followed, all of us together in 2001, as long as they are unwilling or unable to see what we did wrong, no effective remedy will be devised. Then, in the power struggle between America and China, we will fail just as Trump's earlier tariff war did. Meanwhile, China's leaders sit back quietly, and President Xi Jinping smiles. China is steadily getting richer and richer.

Action-reaction

From the Netherlands, where this book originates, it is difficult to assess what is being thought up in Washington, but it does not look like the Washington trade specialists are even starting to consider stopping free trade as a possibility.

All in all, the future of the independence of Western societies hangs by a side thread that US President Donald Trump has in his hands. The very little we Dutch can do is share our views with our US friends. Being allowed to think along with the country that is on our side and strongest there, is the highest achievable thing for the time being, next to that other activity, sailing with our naval ships, together with the Americans in through the Taiwan strait. The Germans do that, too, now. Schulte Nordholt says it well: promoting awareness and, above all, not remaining silent is what we can do.

Unfortunately, The Hague, that is, the Netherlands' government, seems to be stuck with its boots deep in the mud. It does not even want to think about China's danger. And neither the EU nor the United States really see the slowly unfolding disaster for what it is. Nout Wellink, the former President of the Dutch National Bank, seems to be right: soon, the US will just dangle behind China.

*****

Chapter 5

Who continued the Clinton mistake?

First, is China to blame for anything?

China has amassed its huge liquid assets in a very short time, in 23 years, and has already spent three-quarters of these, but in doing so, it is not doing anything wrong. If their political adversaries and business partners are sleeping and making mistakes, like we did and still do, they would be foolish not to take advantage. Although Beijing certainly cheats in other fields, the root cause of China's current enrichment is the free trade agreement that we were stupid enough to initiate. It is, therefore, our responsibility to rectify this error.

What we should have done was not to allow China to trade with us on other than equal terms; in other words, to have agreed that, measured in amounts of money, there should be rough equality in the amounts of goods imported and exported to and from China. That sounds simple, but regulating this in practice would have been something entirely new in international trade. It would have required a new set of organisms to control trade volumes in the US and in the European Union, just for the purpose of keeping this balance. Properly regulated, that would have avoided the current imbalance and we would have had an adequate system from the beginning in 2001. We did nothing of the sort.

Underlying this reasoning is a rule, simple, but still not widely accepted:

Statement 4: A country - or group of countries - should only trade freely with another country if it is not harmed by such free trade.

Free trade with China is beginning to harm us to our core.

*****

Even though China is very dishonest in other matters..

In many ways, China flouts international rules. It does so, e.g., by requesting that subsidiaries from foreign companies be allowed only if they would be 51% Chinese-owned. Thus, the Chinese have been able to steal patents and know-how and transfer them to 100% Chinese-owned companies set up near our subsidies for that purpose. China also did not abide by patent and trademark rules for years. Patent protection allows research to be profitable for the researcher or research company. Patents and trademarks are one of the foundations of our market system, which China has now joined, but without respecting its rules. Only now, after years of theft, trademarks are finally being respected by Beijing, but patents are still only respected where it suits them. Not respecting those rules has given China a huge advantage. When Beijing is challenged on these issues, it often promises that all this will change, but then often continues on its old, unfair footing. This amounts to stealing. China deserves to be stopped with a firm hand.

These Chinese attitudes and methods have a significant negative impact on our economies, but they still pose a far lesser threat than the massive enrichment from free trade.

Where did the fault lie?

Please allow me some fun here and let you read up about the 'Peter Principle'. Here is the URL.

https://en.wikipedia.org/wiki/Laurence_J._Peter.

This theory is both amusing and very realistic. Its concept was first formulated in 1969 by Canadian Laurence J. Peter, and states that employees are regularly promoted on the basis of their past performance, until they eventually reach a level at which they are completely incompetent and then stay in that position for many years. A witty take on an often-seen reality. Whether this concept is also applicable to some of the major players in this free trade we have with China, just take a look at Mr. Pascal Lamy, hereafter.

But if the fault is really ours, who then should have seen the mistake and should have sounded the alarm? Where was the incompetence that still now keeps us in this situation? Who is responsible, and where was the blindness?

Three parties played a role.

- First, the responsibility lies with our political leaders and their advisers. Things often go wrong at a high level.

- Second, there is the horde of journalists, writers of background articles and opinions, the think tanks in the US and in Europe and all the professors of macro-economy at Western universities. For too long, a foolish euphoria prevailed. Where were the bright thinkers? Nowhere! And that is kind of shocking.

- Third and not least, there are the international professionals whose job it is to advise governments on trade and on the consequences of what is being prepared under their watch. They are the men and women of the Geneva-based World Trade Organization, the world's top trade body. How did these supposed professionals fulfill their role? On closer inspection, we find complete incompetence at the WTO.!

Ex-WTO director-general Pascal Lamy, the top incompetent

Pascal Lamy was Director-General of the World Trade Organisation WTO in Geneva from 2005 to 2013. China had joined the WTO in 2001.

Pascal Lamy

During Mr Lamy's tenure, it became inescapably clear that China was enriching itself incredibly fast, see chart in Chapter 1. Mr. Lamy had previously been the right-hand man of Jacques Delors, often recognised as the best-ever European Commission president, and after that, was the European Union trade commissioner from 1999 to 2004. He was, therefore, considered ideally suited for the subsequent WTO job. But this man, during his eight years at the world's top trade advisory organization, never realized the lopsided trade situation the WTO had entered, resulting from 500 million cheap Chinese workers and a dictatorship? Never. In speeches that can still be found on the internet, he just kept touting the virtues of free trade. He often travelled to China, where he was praised, feted and dined, and he loved it.

If we should not be too hard on President Clinton, as he is not an economist himself, nor a trade specialist, we should point the finger at this Frenchman Mr. Pascal Lamy, who was in function as the world's top trade specialist over the crucial period when things started to go wrong. He is the real culprit. What damage has this contentedly smiling man done, who is still undeservedly revered in his native France! This man, in an incredible silly way, oversaw and accepted the present decline of our society.

*****

Too many questions remain unanswered in the press and also by our politicians.

Let's come back to the second group, the press. Stupid statements about China on TV and in the press are customary.

Pretentious 'wise' answers are given to oversimplified questions. Opinions about the future are often full of wishful thinking, and what has made Beijing so powerful in such a short time remains unexplained, even though the facts are clear.

There certainly is good reporting about single aspects of Chinese activity in some parts of the world, especially when there is a new element that the writer has 'discovered'. This then comes across well, but the overall picture, of which such aspect is only a part, is always forgotten. Journalism tends to describe fragments but not the whole pattern they are part of. For readers it is like watching isolated images instead of the full movie.

*****

The questions to be answered.

In both the US and Europe, the press and writers are generally unable to ask the relevant questions, let alone answer them with a comprehensive strategic concept.

1. Is China's growth an inevitable historical event that we should just accept, or are that growth and its consequences man-made with a basic flaw?

2. Does China's military takeover of the South China Sea, which barely borders China, have anything to do with the other questions, or is this a separate issue?

3. Does the cruelty of the Communist Party in Beijing have any importance for us, or is it only of importance for the Chinese people itself and for Tibet? Is it better to ignore, forgive and forget what happens there or should it, on the contrary, shape the overall attitude of our governments towards China?

4. What are our European, UK and American governments and parliaments doing with these questions?

*****

At the end of this chapter, the following must once again be rectified. People still think, "A nation's economic power on the world stage can be measured by the size of its Gross National

Product." But that seems just not right. I think it is the available amount of liquid money that gives power. This fallacy about the effect of the size of GDP lulls us to sleep. With the US and EU GDP's still large, we think all is not so bad.

*****

Chapter 6

Free trade and What It Does to China.

The free trade fallacy

Already in 1986, John M. Culbertson †, an eminent US economist, predicted in an article "The folly of free trade", I quote, "Any manager who tries to create a strategy out of worn-out clichés and unexamined nostrums is dismissed. Yet, in the United States and other Western countries, we have grown comfortable with the government following outworn nostrums about free trade. We have elevated the economic theory of free trade to the status of a national theology, and we follow its simple dictums as if they were immutable laws. We appear prepared to follow the precepts of free trade wherever they lead us, even if that means plunging lemminglike to our economic ruin.". Unquote.

His prediction is coming true, but with a variance. It is not our economic ruin; it is China's economic superiority that is the result. Our ruin just follows. But this man, John Culbertson, saw the idiocy of free trade taken as almost a religion, and saw it right.

Free trade has long been seen as a sacred cow that should never be criticized, but that opinion is finally losing ground. Some writers already have doubts about free trade, but they still only focus on a few cases where some stakeholders have a disadvantage.

Lawrence Mishel, for example, of the Economic Policy Institute, a Washington-based think tank, writes, "The winners have never tried to fully compensate the losers, so let's stop claiming that trade benefits us all." And he means groups of low-skilled workers in developed countries.

The stronger argument, still ignored by most economists, is that with free trade, some economic factors can lead a country, like China now, to become outrageously rich and amass economic power far too quickly, at the expense of its trading partner(s). The first major economist to say this correctly, even though still much too cautiously, is the former IMF chief economist, now its first deputy managing director, PhD Gita Gopinath, as she did in an interview on CNN. The url is https://www.pbs.org/wnet/amanpour-and-company/video/gita-gopinath-discusses-the-state-of-the-global-economy/

(please check between minutes 2:35 and 3: 35 in this video).

The origin of the fallacy

Starting around 1960, the US successfully pushed the concept of free trade for over five decades. This positive information made people everywhere believe that free trade was an ideal. One thought: "Free trade is good, full stop". The argument in a discussion where people say "I am for free trade" today still serves to end a discussion. And so, now that, for the first time in history, a free trade situation is really harmful, many still do not want to know. The truth is that when free trade deeply harms one of the parties involved, it is both fair and necessary between those parties to curtail or even stop that free exchange.

This insight, so full of simple common sense, is still vehemently denied in many circles. Sacred cows don't die easily. But free trade is not an ideal, it is just one of many possible ways to regulate trade between countries. One can choose one option or another. Certainly, until recently, free trade brought much good and little harm everywhere. But for 24 years now, there is this other, big situation which is upsetting the world balance. Continuing to think of free trade as an ideal is primitive. But this idea of "free trade is always good" has taken root so deeply that it is still difficult to turn people away from it.

Only once the realities of free trade are fully understood, can the U.S.—and later, we in Europe—begin developing a more effective strategy toward China.

Neither the White House nor the press are yet able to articulate what is really our problem with China. that. Please, dear reader, read yet again in Chapter 1 the fallacies articulated by President Clinton, on which the entire current free trade with China is based. The present inability to define the problem in this year 2025 is again a lack of clear thinking, just as foolish in itself as President Clinton's error of 23 years ago.

So, let me try to formulate what I criticize others for not doing.

Our mistake with China

The current fallacy with China is that we still do not recognize that, with our money - the money we pay for the $870 billion a year of goods we buy from China more than they buy from us - we are financing the rapid growth of China's gigantic economy, that we are thus supporting our disruptive enemy without even thinking about ending that financial support, nor in what way that could possibly be done. We simply do not want to see the economic-financial reality. By the way, "we" here refers to all countries outside China, which includes together with the US (population 335 billion) and the EU (450 billion) all the other countries that provide a total population of more than a trillion.

*****

The Beijing dictatorship keeps China's labor force poor, even though it is a good thing that the greatest part is now just above the official poverty line.

Before 2001, part of the moral justification for global free trade was the growth of workers' income in a poor country. You help poor people raise their standard of living, and your own country suffers no great disadvantage, often even an advantage. But in China, the size of the poor population combined with the brutality of the party dictatorship distorts this situation: their huge labor force is very cheap and is cruelly being kept that way for as long as possible. In China, this is easy: there are so many of these low-paid laborers. If one group demands more, the government can simply turn to another. While China has certainly already built up a substantial middle class, make no mistake, that is a different group. With dictatorial power, workers in the Chinese factories and shops where cheap products are being produced are kept strictly separate from the new richer middle class. And so, contrary to the wishful thinking of many, the trade will not gradually even out the skewed situation of low production costs.

When our Western press reports that wages in China are now rising, like, for example, in Shenzhen, this is a true detail in itself, but the only important information there is that China still has these huge numbers of workers at its disposal who are much cheaper than our workers in the West, see Chapter 1. China proudly boasts that it has pulled hundreds of millions over the poverty line, but despite this, trade volumes in and out of China remain as uneven as before. China's vast enrichment is continuing at full speed, year after year.

This following little set of figures shows the current skewed trade situation: 83 countries have the European Union as their biggest export market, 28 the US, but for only 14, it is China! China simply imports so little because their own prices are so low.

*****

Chapter 7

The Too-Clever Chinese

During my exhaustive study, I found there is, in the US, a strangely biased habit of writing in favor of China.

In the years after 2021, I still did not understand why, e.g., among the Brookings Institution's publications on China, as soon as the subject matter was important, the writing seemed to be either pro-China, or argumented something like "China will collapse soon," or "Xi Jinping will soon lose power!" Now, the Brookings Institution, the major think tank of the US Democratic Party, is a highly regarded, large institution with more than 900 people working there. I then tried to find the person at Brookings who oversaw the China desk, in order to ask him or her why writing about China regularly minimized the threat China poses for us and regularly kept predicting China's demise, even while that demise just never happens. But I then found that the person overseeing the China desk was a Chinese man, born in Shanghai, having first studied in China. That immediately made me suspicious, and I decided not to contact him but to dig further. That was the beginning of my discovery of a 5th column. The term **"fifth column"** refers to a group of people who secretly undermine a larger group or nation from within, often in favor of an external enemy. Could it be true that there was an underground pro-China movement in the US, cleverly hidden?

A further search yielded more names of China-born authors, who, like this one at Brookings, were making a brilliant career in the US after first having studied in China. Again and again, such men wrote strangely positively about China. I continued to check and found most of these in China born men have now acquired US citizenship. Could this be an organized, secret group, having acquired US citizenship as part of their deception?

I think so. The simple fact that they all write along lines that must please the Communist Party in Beijing, and that there are quite a few of them, all writing in the same sense, that cannot be a coincidence.

The little group of highly educated and talented Chinese-born authors that one easily finds make a brilliant career here and have succeeded in letting the American intellectual world think they are on our side. I here submit that this small group, now all of them with an American passport, fully integrated as they are in the US society, still works for China.

We still ignore that a Chinese person, born in China but now living abroad, inevitably still has family in China, and is therefore under pressure to speak and write positively about the PRC or to predict China's soon-to-be demise. After all, if they can make the US public and US leaders believe this, it makes any US action against China unnecessary, which, of course, will suit Beijing. If such a Chinese man or woman were to do the opposite and write negatively about China or about China's immense, threatening power, he knows that members of his family still residing over there would be in danger. His father, brother or uncle might suddenly lose their jobs, even his very old mother might suddenly be arrested, a grandson or second cousin might suddenly not be admitted to university etc., etc. We still ignore this horrible mechanism, and we gullible Americans and Europeans easily fall for the soothing messages these Chinese publish in the US, about their country of birth.

Another element that, quite independently from the above, makes the existence of this so-called fifth column likely is the experience everyone has had who deals with Chinese who live in the West. After any discussion with negative elements about the PRC regime, the Chinese man or woman we talk to, in a friendly way, will often end the conversation by reverting to an expression of loyal support for the Chinese fatherland. Chinese have a very strong loyalty to their country. To assume this loyalty is high with simple Chinese but much lower with intellectually highly educated ones, like the ones I write about here, is not based on any fact. It is only wishful thinking. Chinese intellectuals can be fiercely loyal to their country of birth and race too.

These Chinese-born Americans, who make a brilliant career in the US and then publish favorably for Beijing, are but a small group — by my estimation, they are less than a dozen.

So, the head of the Chinese desk at Brookings apparently influenced the writing about China of this famous Institution in a way favorable to Beijing,

How have they hidden themselves so well? They have done this by often providing stinging and sharp criticism of China or of the Communist Party, about some non-vital detail or topic, like Beijing's cruelty to the Uigurs, or about the judiciary that is being biased by influence from the communist party. This makes it appear that they are 'against' China. But then, in the articles that are vital, where the issue is whether to warn the American public about China's aggression, they write exactly what Beijing would want them to. Up till now, the American public and the editors that publish their work see them as 'experts about China who are on our side.' I see them, well organized as they are, on China's side.

Should there be any Chinese-born writers who do not write in the interest of the PRC, that would be because these could already have lost their two parents and have no other family over there. But then these few risk alienating their other Chinese friends and are still in danger themselves. A car accident or some other 'mishap' may well happen. That would then be just reported as an accident. 'These Chinese still cannot drive'.

*****

An example

To illustrate the above, I quote a typical text here, published by one of these very successful Chinese. His autobiographical story is quite long, but, in order to report faithfully, I copy it here in full. You will see that this is quite brilliantly done to convince us.

Quote (5 pages long)

I am proud to be an American - by (Chinese name withheld)

I was born in 1960, when China was an integral part of the Soviet coalition that had wrapped the United States in an epic ideological and strategic rivalry called the Cold War. When I was 10, China's great leader Mao Tse Tung issued his famous statement, "People of the world unite and defeat the US imperialists and their running dogs". I was a freshman on 16 December 1978 when the college broadcasting system broadcast the Chinese American Normalization Communiqué. Like everyone else, I was stunned. How could China enter into a relationship with an evil nation we had been trained and taught to overthrow? I was at home celebrating Chinese New Year in 1979 when my family watched Deng Xiaoping's historic visit to the US on a small black-and-white television. We were again stunned by what we saw on the screen: there was no sign of a country crumbling because of capitalist exploitation, racial tensions, nor Wall Street profiteering and political corruption. But because we lived in a country where the media was carefully choreographed to reflect the party's open agenda and where listening to the Voice Of America was considered a crime, it was difficult for us to fathom the significance of these two events at the time. Not long after, American professors arrived on our campus.

Translating American literature and studying in the outer country.

81

In 1982, I graduated from university with a degree in English language and literature and was appointed editor at the provincial publishing house of Shaanxi. My professors were able to visit sister universities in the US. When they returned, I would often visit them, go through the books they brought back and decide which books should be translated into Chinese. I had no knowledge of copyright law, and the decision to translate and publish American literary work depended solely on whether it had any academic value and whether it could make a profit. I edited pirated American literary works for more than five years and even translated a few American novels myself. Some of my classmates and colleagues were sent abroad by the government to study, but I was never chosen. After my elder brother returned from a visit to the US organized by the U.S. Information Agency in 1985, he encouraged me to go to the US to study. I hesitated because I felt I would not pass the physical test, since I had also been almost excluded from the Chinese college due to physical disability. On top of that, where would the tuition fees come from if I was admitted? When I learned that no one had to pass a US university to study, I decided to apply anyway.

In August 1987, I arrived at the University of Hawaii in Manoa with two suitcases and $200 in cash. I was to pursue a master's degree in US history. As an assistant, my tuition fees were automatically waived, and there was a monthly stipend. Teaching American students was tough and learning equally difficult, but life was exciting. My intention was to return to China with my master's *degree, but I preferred to pursue a higher degree in US diplomatic history. I applied to several graduate schools and was admitted to all of them. I decided to go to Emory University because it offered me a Robert W. Woodruff Fellowship given annually to about 12 doctoral students. It meant I would get $1,000 a month for four years without working. Since Woodruff was one of the leaders of the rise of the Coca-Cola Company, when I set foot on the Emory campus in August 1989, I made the decision to stop drinking Pepsi. Over the years, I have encouraged my family members and my students to do the same.*

Volunteering for the Carter election project

Centre for Chinese Villages

In the autumn of 1996, I was teaching American history at DeKalb College when one of my professors at Emory, Dr Robert Pastor, sent me an e-mail and asked if I could help him learn more about Chinese village elections. I told him that Chinese villages had no elections. I was clearly wrong, because Chinese villages began holding elections in 1988 under a provisional law, and the Carter Center was invited to observe these elections, which were held every three years in nearly a million villages in China. I started volunteering for the Carter Center's project on Chinese village elections. I first met President Carter in October 1996 when I was an observer at the Carter Center's election observation in Nicaragua. Two years later, I joined the Carter Centre on a part-time basis. Ten years after he and Deng Xiaoping took the decision to establish full diplomatic engagements, I began working for the man whose courageous and visionary actions forever changed my life, the fate of my native country and the well-being of my adopted nation.

Travelling with President Carter

In 2001, I travelled to China with President Carter for the first time. Since then, I organized all his trips to China until September 2014, when he made his last trip to China at the age of 90. President Carter liked to engage with Chinese university students whenever he was in China. On many such occasions, he would recall very fondly the 3 am phone call he received from his adviser on science, Dr Frank Press, who visited China to discuss US-China scientific exchanges, and he asked the latter to tell Deng Xiaoping that all Chinese students and scholars were welcome in the US (see above letter from President Carter to the Chinese embassy on 21 November 2019)

I have lived in America for more than 32 years now. A thought that keeps coming to my mind is: Could Americans my age (27) go to China, study, have the opportunity to teach and even be able to get a job with one of China's high-ranking leaders? I know there are many Chinese with careers like mine in the U.S. I don't know an American who has done the same in China. If there were, we would certainly know. My work and life in America is a small reflection of the essence of this great nation, a footnote to its domination of political, scientific and academic affairs in the world, and a consolation at this difficult time when there are Americans calling for decoupling with China. Born and raised in China, I am now a proud American. I am both a beneficiary of and witness to the importance of peaceful and productive relations between the U.S. and China. There are millions like me across the Pacific.

End of quote

Here is the URL of the above:

https://usheartlandchina.org/reflections/i-am-proud-to-be-an-american-yawei-liu/ .

I have no doubt that this man has really met President Carter. This story is true, he is clearly brilliant. But he still writes what Beijing wants him to write! A beautiful text like this is exactly what honest and good-willing Americans fall for. I could not trace the date of this writing, it is probably several years old, but I became convinced this is a deception when, on June 3d, 2022, this same Chinese author published the article "Decoupling between the U.S. and China May be as Disruptive as COVID-19 " [13], because this article says exactly what Beijing wants the Americans to believe. Not to decouple is pro-PRC writing. The average American reader thinks this article gives a valuable assessment by a well-meaning

---

[13] https://usheartlandchina.org/reflections/i-am-proud-to-be-an-american-yawei-liu/

Chinese, now a naturalized American, who is on our side. In truth, though, 'decoupling' is the last thing Beijing wants the US to do because it would violently reduce the $870 billion annually that enters China's coffers. And by writing like this, this Chinese is probably protecting his family in China from terrible measures.

From the above, together with a few similar writings, I conclude that this Chinese author is one of the little groups actively influencing American public opinion, loyal to Beijing.

*****

All this too positive writing about China, always in the real interest of Beijing, always by a Chinese who was born in China — often in Shanghai, by the way — who always first studied at a university in China, then has gotten a PhD in the US, then always is making a brilliant career here, always negative on China when the subject is not essential, so as to pretend being anti-PRC, and always writing in the interest of Beijing when it can influence US strategic thinking about China, all this writing, not by just one man but by a small group of writing Chinese in the US, now all of them having US citizenship, THAT CANNOT BE A COINCIDENCE.

Coincidences exist; we all come across them, but here, we see too many 'coincidences', all pointing in the same direction. That eliminates the possibility of coincidence. It cannot be other than a managed occurrence and gives – in my opinion - proof of this very successful and very well-hidden Chinese fifth column in the US.

And what we see is extraordinary. For example, there is this dissident Chinese woman who was expelled from the party, was able to leave China, and now lives in the US. Nobody doubts that she is against the Communist Party in Beijing. But what she publishes is exactly what Beijing wants us to believe: Xi Jinping will not last long, she writes! If she were on our side, she would encourage us to stop free trade with China, but she does the opposite; she says, "No sweat, Xi cannot last". Do I see ghosts, or am I right?

If true, and I have no doubt it is, for China to have been able to influence the publications of the Brookings Institution - the Democrats' think tank! - on China and to have been able to influence general American opinion about China, and then to have managed to keep this activity secret for about 20 years, that is a huge success for Beijing! And it happens not just at Brookings. Foreign Affairs Magazine, so highly regarded, publishes in the same way. We must clean this up. After the publication of this book and this exposure, the next trick we may expect is that some of these Chinese will change their surname into something sounding American. Please beware, they are clever.

Up till recently, the President of the Brookings Institution was a Chinese-born woman called Amy Liu (yes!). This high-ranking and successful American was born in Hong Kong and, therefore, may be somewhat less suspicious. But whether she is pro-Beijing or not, what I write here is, of course, a terrible embarrassment for her. If true, it must even be a terrible embarrassment for the whole 13-person Executive Leadership Team at Brookings. I, therefore, expect strenuous denial, and I expect to be ridiculed as soon as this book comes out. I also expect some of this small group of Chinese-born writers to change jobs quickly now, so as to get themselves out of the limelight. Hopefullu, meanwhile, there will be some Americans of good standing and high intellect who will objectively, thoroughly and professionally investigate what I indicate here.

It is high time we pay more attention to the background of Chinese-born authors and check what they write, because this kind of insidious influence on US political opinion contributes to the US not taking the political measures we would otherwise take to protect our society from China's influence. Right now, we are just letting things happen.

*****

Chapter 8

Dictatorship or democracy?

With the US still leading our whole Western world, we face a difficult, indeed Churchillian choice. The perceived fifth column, influencing general opinion, is but one element. The real danger comes from China's enrichment.

Either we sleepily let the current trade relationship with China simmer on, which means that we quietly hand over world power to Beijing. In that case - as Dutch Professor Rob de Wijk puts it - we can soon forget about our free-market economy, international law, international institutions, democracy, human rights and civil liberties, both in the US and in Europe.

The alternative is, under US leadership, we end free trade with China that was started in 2001 on such totally wrong grounds, and we put the most important power relationship in the world on a sound footing. This may be one of the most difficult activities ever to regulate, but if we do it, we preserve our freedoms and self-reliance for the future, those values we have fought so hard for over the centuries.

That is the choice we face, and I very much fear we will not do it right.

*****

Chapter 9

Decision makers

The spirit of some major world thinkers plays a role in the subject of this book.:

Deng Xiaoping, who managed to transform China's domestic economy from Marxist state ownership to private ownership and - so important - competition. A herculean task, carried out swiftly and successfully by this man of genius. See Chapter 12 for more details about this man.

John Maynard Keynes, who explained to us the functioning of a country's economy. Without his insight, we would not be able to understand the dangerous aspect of free trade with low-cost China.

Winston Churchill, who faced a choice at the beginning of the Second World War - to fight or not to fight - which he managed to make and then famously stuck to. Can we make this equally difficult choice with China - namely, to stop that free trade - or are we too weak? Only the US can initiate this, and I fear she will not.

Henry Kissinger, who, just before he died once more, gave his five decades old opinion that the US and China should eventually find a way to coexist peacefully. I would agree with Mr. Kissinger, but I think that we will only succeed if we take away the ease with which we allow China to become the world superpower: End Free trade. Mr. Kissinger did not see that this trade disequilibrates the world. Rather than seeing present reality, he stuck to what he already had said half a century ago.

Albert Einstein observed that people's stupidity is infinite. Could we, for once, make an exception to that 'observation', be clever and get out of the present trap??

*****

Keynes and financially trained politicians

There is something interesting to observe about distrust among financiers. It is still quite common to see Keynes' theory dismissed by financiers as something dangerous, incorrect, or at least suspect.

The German Minister of Finance Wolfgang Schäuble, who, as the predecessor of Dijsselbloem, had his hands on the EU purse strings when it came to spending the European financial aid to Greece, refused to see that his demand for austerity by Athens would harm Greek GDP, as any Keynesian could have told him. Schäuble was so strict that Greek GNP then fell by 25%. A gigantic error, which he still has not acknowledged. A 25% cut in GDP, poor Greece! Yanis Varoufakis, outstanding Greek finance minister at the time, lost the discussion he started about this, and Schäuble continued.

ECB (The European Central Bank) President Jean-Claude Trichet believed that only austerity would restore confidence in the economy. Had his successor Mario Draghi not done the opposite, that is, starting to liberally spend money, the Euro would most likely have gone under. With Draghi's famous 'As Much As It Takes", Mr. Trichet lost face for the rest of his career.

Onno Ruding, former Dutch Minister of Finance who famously put the Dutch finances in order, surely a great man, in conversations with me a few years ago, closed our discussion with emphasis and authority by saying that what Keynes claimed could not be trusted anyway. I had to make do with that.

Many financiers still think like this because, for them, Keynes inverses right and wrong. And he does in a sense, because he says that in an economic crisis, a government should consider spending more instead of less. That is anathema to an old-fashioned financier. That cannot be right, is their instinct, because in a crisis, a financier has learned to reduce spending. Mario Draghi is one of the very exceptional financiers who fully understood Keynes, but then he studied at M.I.T., one of the few universities where Keynes' theory is being taught well, including to students at the finance faculty.

Financially educated people often still do not accept the excellent teachings of Keynes. It is high time that changed.

*****

PART TWO

This part has two aspects: first, a few practical assessments of Taiwan and China and second, a the discussion philosophical and historical aspect that surrounds the situation described in Part One.

Chapter 10

Taiwan and its safety.

A. Who speaks about the danger coming from China, speaks about Taiwan.

There are three reasons for the US to protect Taiwan from a Chinese takeover.

The first is surely that we, out of decency, should not let a well-run democracy of 23 million people fall into the hands of an aggressive neighboring dictatorship. That would be very callous, and no other Asiatic country would trust us anymore if we allowed it. And even though this book devotes little space to it, simply protecting these 23 million inhabitants in their democracy, is that not the most decent and important argument?

Taiwan, as it is run now, proves that the Chinese PRC argument that "The Chinese people, because of their nature, need a strict, centralized dictatorship" is total nonsense. With its Chinese population, Taiwan is a vibrant democracy, politically sound, robust and extremely successful businesswise. For Beijing, which claims that democracy is a decadent system, Taiwan is the nearby and inconvenient proof of the contrary. Taiwan's status and the free speech that reigns there do not just irritate Beijing. Like any dictatorship, Beijing fears that the strong, positive happiness given by freedom of speech may well blow over to the mainland from across the Taiwan Strait and undermine their cruel regime.

The second reason to protect Taiwan is its symbolic function. Protected or swallowed up by China, Taiwan's fate will have a huge impact on surrounding countries, on the Philippines, Indonesia, on Japan, and especially on the small, weaker countries such as Vietnam, Laos, Cambodia, Malaysia, etc. If Taiwan were taken over by China, all the surrounding countries would know that China's power is so great that they must comply with China's aggressive wishes. If, however, it becomes increasingly clear that Taiwan is protected by the US and Japan, then that gives all surrounding countries a reason to rely on the US, on democracy and generally on the West. President Biden understood this second aspect very well. As far as I can fathom, President Trump understands this strategic position well too.

But there is a third, even stronger reason we cannot let Taiwan fall into China's hands. That is the existence of the Taiwanese chip industry, which supplies roughly half of all chips in the world and, moreover, has top-level research and development. Should this industry fall into Beijing's hands, the entire manufacturing world in the US, in the EU and elsewhere would become dependent on China for chips. We obviously cannot run that risk, so the US *must* protect Taiwan! Simultaneously though, seeing that horrible risk, the US is investing hugely in chip manufacture, with the help of Taiwan!

The major remaining risk for Taiwan is the passage of time. If we let free trade with China continue, China's far too rapid growth will continue inevitably, and a time will come when China will be stronger than the US both economically, but also militarily because it is going to be able to pour greater money into research for more modern weapons. With continued free trade, inevitably, the money will keep flowing. In probably between 10 and 20 years, the Beijing government will then simply be able to take the island and a relatively weaker US will not be unable to stop that.

China can only grow so fast because of free trade with us. That trade has to end.

*****

Taiwan plays an important role in the global power struggle that is now beginning to heat up.

*****

Why did the West ever subscribe to China's one-country concept?

Until recently, the fate of Taiwan was unclear. There was a carefully maintained doubt, called the 'One-China-concept', that gave the aggressive regime in Beijing the illusion that it could eventually take Taiwan by military or other means of pressure. President Joe Biden, who appeared to be an excellent strategist, realized that this doubt would only lead to misunderstandings. When, on three different occasions, a journalist - not the same one each time, by the way - asked him whether the US would defend Taiwan if it were attacked by China, he answered with a short 'yes' every time, briefly but firmly. This new position of the US was seized upon by Nancy Pelosi to include Taiwan on her August 2022 eastern tour.

Finally, in September 2022, when asked for the fourth time, President Joe Biden confirmed that, in case of a Chinese attack, the US would defend Taiwan and that the US would deploy ground troops.

History of the One-country Policy

The decision by the US to commit itself, in the Shanghai Communique of 1972, to the PRC's idea of a one-China-concept was made shortly after China started its contact with the West. The US wanted to please China, which had still somewhat uncomfortably 'opened up', with the thought, "Let us not immediately refuse bluntly on this issue which is emotionally important to them". The political thought behind this, in my eyes, was "if we are unfriendly now, we will get unfriendliness back later; if we are friendly now, we will be able to cooperate on good terms later. China will also gradually understand that".

China, however, has reacted in exactly the opposite way, becoming increasingly aggressive — especially in recent years under Xi Jinping. Or in other words, China ignored the hand of friendship extended by the West at the time. Noting this, Joe Biden, while now clear about his military defense of Taiwan, nevertheless told Xi again on November 14, 2022, in Bali, that he still holds on to the one-China position. A curious concession to Beijing in words, which is, of course, in direct contradiction to his words about the defense of Taiwan.

Mr. Kissinger sees this differently. See Chapter 6.

And yes, I do not take political sides, but professionally, I was impressed by Joe Biden's strategic thinking, while unhappy about his free trade blindness. That issue is being much betterg understood by President Trump.

*****

C. The importance of Taiwan's chip industry

Here are some statistics on Taiwan's global position. If you do not like numbers and graphs, just skip this section.

Taiwan is home to the world's largest and third-largest chip manufacturers, TSMC and UMC. TSMC recently held 53% of world sales, UMC 18%, so together 71%!

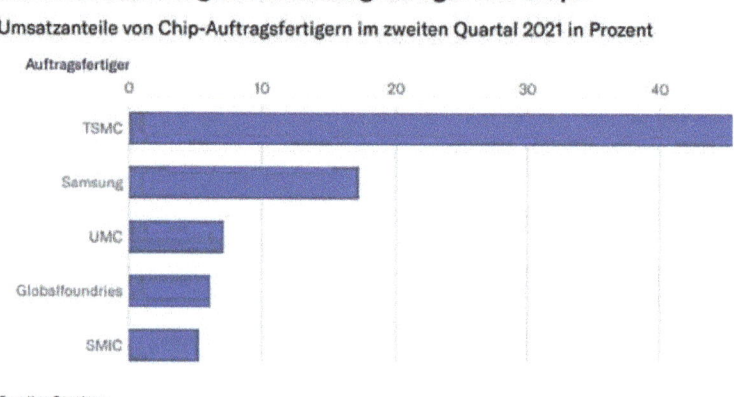

TSMC ist klar der grösste Auftragsfertiger von Chips

Umsatzanteile von Chip-Auftragsfertigern im zweiten Quartal 2021 in Prozent

Quelle: Statista

TSMC, Taiwan Semiconductor Manufacturing Company, has become known to a wider public in the wake of the ongoing chip shortage and is undisputedly the largest and the technological leader, ahead of South Korea's Samsung. Apple, Tesla, AMD and Nvidia have all their best chips for smartphones, laptops, e-cars and graphics cards produced at TSMC.

Also located in Taiwan is the world's largest chip assembly and testing company, ASE. Unknown to the general public, ASE is the world market leader in its field, with a 25 per cent world market share.

And the third-largest manufacturer of wafers, the pizza-shaped silicon disks from which chips are made, is also based on the island.

Apple ist mit Abstand der wichtigste Kunde von TSMC

Grösste TSMC-Kunden im Jahr 2021, geschätzte Umsatzanteile in Prozent

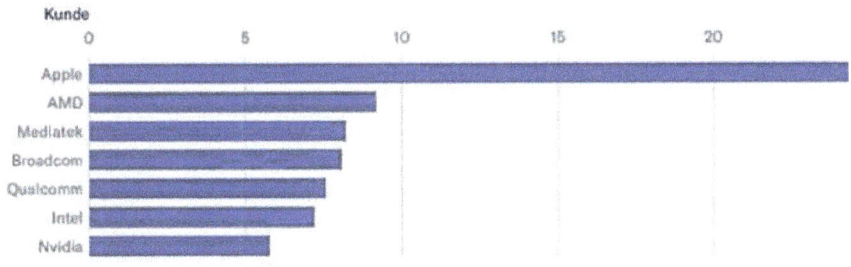

Quelle: The Information Network / Seeking Alpha   NZZ

In the field of chip design, it is the US that is by far the largest in the world, with 26%, and Taiwan in second place with 9%. (Source: the Berlin-based 'Stiftung Neue Verantwortung').

Finally - and this is less well known – Taiwan is an important place for substrates and laminates with which silicon is coated. Many of these chemical materials are not even produced in this quantity and with this purity in Europe. However, European companies also produce in Taiwan. For example, according to a spokesperson in Guanyin near Taipei, Germany's BASF produces "chemicals for the highest demands of the semiconductor industry, primarily to lend to local customers in Taiwan".

In short, Taiwan is the most versatile chip-making hub in the world. Its strength comes not only from a few large companies, but much more from the unique density of this cluster, which also includes many small, unknown suppliers. An industry source revealed, "If you look at the market segment for processor chips, from basic Intel x86 processors to high-end processors for smartphones, today about 80 per cent goes through Taiwan." Corresponding industrial parks stretch from the north to the south of the island - on the west side facing China. Foreign chip suppliers are also expanding further in Taiwan such as German specialty materials manufacturer Merck.

Because the US, and eventually all industrialized countries, are so economically and technologically dependent on TSMC and Co, the US will try to keep China from invading for that reason alone. The Taiwanese government knows this, of course, and is steadily strengthening its 'silicon shield', a household word in Taiwan.

Nancy Pelosi's controversial visit to Taiwan this summer, in my view, was a necessary message to China, saying: "We will never give in to threats". Shortly before traveling, at

https://www.washingtonpost.com/opinions/2022/08/02/nancy-pelosi-taiwan-visit-op-ed/, she had given her arguments in no uncertain terms.

*****

Chapter 11

Will Beijing Support Moscow?

At the war in Ukraine, one of the current dangers for us is China's possible financial support for Putin. After some time, the Russians might not be able to sustain the fight with Ukraine due to lack of money. China can mitigate that risk because China has endless money. Such support would be a setback for Ukraine and, thus, for us.

Up till recently, Moscow was still hardly feeling the consequences. Russia instead sells oil to India and to China, among others, even if at heavily discounted prices.

These exports to Asia actually increased Russia's oil revenue by $1.7 billion (€1.6 billion) in May 2022 compared to April '22. And this contributed to the Ruble being the world's strongest-performing currency in June 2022.

The price Russia now gets per barrel may have been reduced by about $30, but Putin, because of the volume of it going to India, and other countries, is getting in quite a bit of money.

In addition, in February 2022, it was decided to build the 'Soyuz Vostok, ' a gas pipeline through Mongolia to China with a capacity of 50 million^{m3}.

But the messages that Russian economy and its society are paying a near unsustainable price for the war are increasing.

These two dictatorships have a common interest in keeping

countries where free expression of opinion is allowed as far away from their borders as they can. They fear the idea of free speech may undermine their oppressive dictatures. It is, therefore, likely that Beijing will increasingly support Putin, and that means Ukraine will have to keep fighting hard. Only if Putin were to lose very clearly would Beijing perhaps refrain from helping him. In this, the Chinese have an opposite interest: they want to be seen as peaceful and friendly by African heads of state. That, too, is important to them. Their support for Putin, therefore, depends on what they consider more important at any given moment: their fighting together against democracies or their global reputation.

Right now, March 2025, China seems to abstain, which would indicate they think their reputation is more important to them than helping the Putin brother-dictatorship.

Chapter 12

Europe Is Still Too Weak

A country or a group of countries is sometimes hampered by its own rules. That is happening in the European Union.

Long ago, China was hampered by its own rules, too. In the 15th century, the Ming emperors suddenly forbade all travel abroad and after the year 1433, they had all 3,500 existing Chinese sea-going wooden ships burned. That stopped China's global expansion, which would otherwise have made history.

And now, the EU is similarly hampered by one of its own rules: the requirement of unanimity among the member states. As it is, each EU member state has a veto right, that can block the actions of the European Commission (EC) in its foreign policy. Recently, it was Hungary's PM Vikter Orban who wished to block the European Commission. The origin of that veto rule is understandable. The European Union was created in a series of agreements between member countries. At the time of signing the final Lisbon Treaty in 2007, each country still wished to retain its sovereignty, meaning they wanted to be able to veto anything that was being concocted in Brussels that would involve them and with which they would disagree, hence the rule of unanimity. But that being so, everyone will understand that such a rule cripples efficient governance. Guy Verhofstadt, former prime minister of Belgium and now head of the Liberal Group in the European Parliament, once said, "In a world dominated by the Chinese empire, India, the Americans and the Russian Federation, do you want us to meet four times a year and make unanimous decisions with the 27 members? That will never work."

See also chapter 3. Greece has received a large money inflow from China. Using its veto, three times already, Greece has killed a measure the EC wanted to take vis-à-vis China. This means that, due to this veto right, the Commission can not protect its own strongest asset, the European single market.

Another example of this crippling unanimity rule was described in the EU-observer of 20 March 2018.

quote

"Five eastern European states prevent new CAP (= Common Agricultural Policy) consensus. . This statement was only supported by 23 out of 28 member states, as Estonia, Latvia, Lithuania, Poland and Slovakia are unsatisfied with relatively lower per-hectare payments to farmers."

end quote

Again, the EC was stopped. But if the Commission were to ask to abolish the unanimity rule, many of the 27 member states would most likely not want to give up their veto right. Not only Greece, but most ex-Soviet satellite countries would refuse, including Poland, Hungary, Romania, Bulgaria, Slovenia, Bosnia, Croatia, and maybe even one or two Baltic states.

In order to have the EU governed efficiently, a quantified voting rule could be adopted for each subject (agriculture, the military, cyber-security and all other subjects), each time adapted to the current situation among the member states. Sometimes, a simple majority would be good, sometimes a 2/3 majority, and in some cases, another voting rule, such as "only when two members wish to vetoe". But establishing these rules with all 27 members would require extensive political negotiations, subject to subject. That would take a lot of time, time we do not have. After all, there are many other topics that precisely need to be urgently dealt with!

The only way to quickly end this weakening veto power then seems to be the creation of a two-speed Europe, such as originally proposed by Jacques Delors in 2013[14], more recently by then Italian PM. Mario Draghi and recently by President Macron. Even if only a nucleus of six countries, say the Netherlands, Belgium, Luxembourg, Germany, France and Italy, were to unite in this way, such a nucleus could adopt a qualified majority rule among itself. Then, when necessary, the Commission could act efficiently on behalf of such a core group. Other EU member states could always join that core, and many would wish to join, in order to belong to

---

[14] Delors: 'I think that countries that want to go further in sharing sovereignty should do so. My wish is that there should be two coherent and distinct groupings: one made up of the vanguard countries that would go further in sharing sovereignty, and the other made up of the newcomers. Of course, the group formed by the vanguard countries would be open to those who wished to join if they met the necessary conditions for entry.

that inner circle group that would make the important decisions. At the moment, however, we are not moving in that direction at all. The idea of a core group and majority rule among these is at a standstill.

Apart from the rule of unanimity, what else stands in Europe's way?

- The endless Brexit negotiations took up too much of our leaders' precious time and attention, but they are over.

- There are still right-wing politicians who want to take their country out of the EU. That is wrong thinking.

- Hungarian Prime Minister Viktor Urban, playing the strong man, does not understand the need for the EU to be efficient. Etc.

Fortunately, not everything is negative. It is already quite a feat that politicians from so many countries, with so many different languages, cultures and backgrounds can work together peacefully in Brussels and so increase the strength of the European Union step by step. And then there are also good people among our politicians.

One of the clearest views on what we should do came on May 16, 2018, from Poland's Donald Tusk, then president of the European Council, when he gave the opening speech at the dinner of the six-month Bulgarian EU presidency in Bucharest, with all EU leaders around the table. "I have no doubt", he said, "that in the new global game, Europe will either be one of the most important players or a pawn. That is the only real alternative. To be the subject and not the object of world politics, Europe must unite economically, politically and also militarily as never before. Simply put: either we are together, or we are nothing." Mr. Tusk is now Poland's PM.

And if Ursula von der Leijen is doing well, with the only exception of her total lack of economic insight, the most positive develoopent for Euroope has been President Trumps trecent threat he might not help Europoe milkitarily. That has been a real boost for European political will to work and rearm together.

*****

Chapter 13

The Contrast Between Two Important Men Of The Past

A. The man who made China wake up, Deng Xiao Ping.

As mentioned before, in 1978, the highly intelligent Chinese Party leader Deng Xiaoping began to replace the unproductive Marxist economic system with the system of ownership and competition, usually called the "market economy," that we, Europe and the U.S., have developed so successfully over the past centuries. From our thinkers and writers in the West one hardly reads this anymore, but this transformation arguably is the most important macroeconomic event in the world over the last 100 years.

This gigantic transformation was finished around 1994. The entire Marxist economic system and its legislation about market and property was replaced! Beijing executed this shift with remarkable speed and efficiency. While the absence of political opposition, parliamentary debate, and democratic delays allowed the dictatorship to act quickly, the sheer scale of the transformation was still extraordinary. Then, in 1995, in order to gain access to world markets, China applied for membership of the WTO, the World Trade Organization in Geneva. Membership was finally obtained in 2001, thanks to President Clinton's deeply erroneous prediction.

China woke up thanks to the statesman and economic genius Deng Xiaoping.

What he did was famously predicted already in 1973 by the Frenchman Alain Peyrefitte in his book *"Quand la Chine s'éveillera le monde tremblera."* In English: *"When China wakes up, the world will tremble."*

Deng Xiao Ping

*****

B. How Henry Kissinger ignored reality on the ground.

He was a very impressive man and his opinions, unchanged over 50 years, have strongly influenced American thinking, but his opinion recently turned out to be questionable.

Ever since 1972, when he traveled to China with President Nixon, he has said the US and China must find a peaceful way together, and he has kept saying this over the next half-century.

Shortly before his death, on October 24, 2023, he said again, *"I believe now as I believed 50 years ago that relations depend on an understanding that the two countries have a unique ability to bring peace and progress to the world and also a unique ability to destroy the world if they are not together."* Deeply anchored in Mr. Kissinger's view was his idea of the very positive human nature of politicians, both at home and in China. He thought that, in the end, politicians are reasonable.

Mr. Kissinger also said and wrote that the US had committed to the 'One China policy' and should keep its word.

I feel Mr. Kissinger has consistently ignored two important facts. The first is that China keeps being aggressive, which precludes the understanding Mr. Kissinger wished. Second is that with the major error by President Clinton in the year 2000, we are enriching China, and with this enrichment we are actually encouraging Beijing to be aggressive. Any understanding like Mr. Kissinger wished for can only start after we stop making it too easy for them to be aggressive. That is, free trade must be ended before China will ever consider peaceful coexistence.

Had Winston Churchill given in to Hitler's aggressivity, the world would have become a bad place. In the same vein, China's too-fast economic growth must be stopped; it must not be accepted, but we are doing that now.

Chapter 14

One of the Historic Origins of Our Political Control

This chapter is not a succession to the previous chapters. It gives a look at a faraway past.

Our ethics, our laws and our philosophical backgrounds are rooted in what is called the Judeo-Christian tradition.

If we then take a glance at the ten centuries before the year zero of our calendar, we see that in Israel, a succession of prophets not only spoke the word of their god, but also did something quite different from what people did with power in other countries at the time: the Israelis systematically criticized the government in their land; they dared tell one king after another what he was doing wrong, often even threatening him with the wrath and punishment of their god. This is in sharp contrast with records written in the same period about all other regimes, the kings of Babylon, the pharaohs, emperors, generals, etc., all of whom had to be praised and listened to. Criticizing in these other lands was out of the question.

These unique Jewish checks on their own government, then, are perhaps the earlier mindset from which our Western democracies originate, even before he so often touted Greek democracy. We accept — or rather we demand — control over political power in our countries, and we have this control through our parliaments, our courts, our free speech, our journalism, our strikes, and even our right to demonstrate. More indirectly, one can even argue that our idea of human rights, a typical Western ethical idea, descends from these early customs of controlling Jewish kings for correctness and truth. Our Western political and social functioning — thanks to this control — is a gem. It gives us our so cherished freedom of expression, but it also gives us the accompanying responsibility to protect that freedom.

This freedom is under threat now.

*****

With China's rapidly expanding power, the key question is whether its recent actions pose a threat or simply reflect the natural rise of another global player. This book contends that China's explosive and unsustainably fast growth—fueled by our reckless embrace of free trade—endangers us, and that we should stop helping China grow so ridiculously fast.

Chapter 15

The UK and Its Recent Mess

Brexit, Rishi Sunak and now Keir Starmer.

This has little to do with China, but Britain's lot is part of the future, both of the US and of Europe.

1. David Cameron

When PM, he travelled to Brussels three times, indicating to the British public that he would tell Brussels to abolish the political aspect of the EU. It is a mystery how this man can have thought, simply by coming over and telling them, that Brussels politicians, after having overcome 6 decades of crises with sheer willpower, would ever abolish any of their so hard-fought results. What statesman's incompetence! The English electorate saw Cameron come back every time with empty hands. They erroneously concluded that Brussels was no good partner for the UK and voted for Brexit. This politically unfit man then returned for a short period as Foreign Secretary under Sunak. This man being returned to a high position indicates the UK Tories were already losing it.

2. Theresa May

Succeeding Cameron, she could have followed her previous opinion that it were best for the UK to 'remain' in the European Union. But, even though she was not legally bound to do so, she respected the referendum outcome. That made the disaster continue.

3. Boris Johnson

As a journalist, previously stationed in Brussels, he had written mocking articles about the EU. None of what he wrote was true, but the simple English public loved it. With these lies, even before he became PM himself, he prepared that small majority in his country for Brexit, with the resulting disaster. That is what Rishi Sunak later inherited.

4. Liz Truss,

With her economic delusions, together with her friend Chancellor of the Exchequer, she created doubt about competence at Downing Street. After only six weeks, she resigned in disgrace.

5. Rishi Sunak

After such under-performing predecessors, it would have seemed easy for Mr. Sunak to do better, but he inherited chaos in the Tory party and, with it, the economic problems. Very positive, though, were his first words when becoming PM. He was cut from the right cloth. Morally, too, he seemeded solid. But the electorate had enough of 14 years of incompetence at the Tories.

6. Keith Starmer

This man clearly is a decent and honest man, and he has reshaped the Labour Party. But he does not have, like Sunak did, much of an idea on how to run the economy. A decent but rather incompetent man? We have to wait and see. Up till now, he seems to do really well, especially in his bringing the whole European Union together on the Ukrainian war.

*****

Addendum 1

An earlier prediction

In March 1991, in the Dutch newspaper NRC. I predicted a general economic debacle and widespread bankruptcies in the former German Democratic Republic (GDR). This was just after the decision to reunite the two Germanies.

The Berlin Wall fell on 9 November 1989. In June 1990, Chancellor Kohl decided that West Germany's strong currency, the Deutsche Mark (DM), would also become the currency for the new federal states, the former GDR. When I read this I wrote a letter to the Dutch newspaper NRC, predicting general bankruptcy in the newly joined German Länder..

Please find here the translated text of the 1991 Dutch language letter:

*****

German error

The East German economic debacle is now well known, but a lot of nonsense is still being written about the cause. What went wrong is due to a fundamental economic mistake made by us. Take any country, communist or not, that is backward in all its economic systems and sub-systems, give it a strong currency and open its borders to imports from strong economies. Then, ANY economic activity in that country will be more expensive or of lower quality than what is produced outside; no one can compete with imports anymore; economic activity will come to a standstill in all sectors – agricultural, construction, heavy industry, light industry, services. And this is now happening in the former GDR. Even when a West German company invests in the eastern provinces, the resulting factory will produce more expensively and/or at high her costs than elsewhere, and for a long time. If the VW group installs a modern engine in the Trabant, the resulting car will be more expensive and/or of lower quality than a car from Western Europe or Czechoslovakia, because at Western cost, people will be used in the production process, people that do not know western efficiency. So what to do then? If wages in East German provinces remain lower than in West Germany, East Germans workers will move to the West. So that won't work. Who then will invest in the former East Germany after the initial enthusiasm wears off? The disaster will be a little slower than described here, and there will be a few exceptions, but the debacle is fundamental and will lead to generalized unemployment, misery, and anger.

If the above is correct, the next question is how such a mistake was possible in the first place. It is probably due to Chancellor Kohl's great haste. In having haste, he was right, but the economic error he made was due to his economic advisers. Nobody warned him. Those who hoped he would pay politically for this economic and human error were disappointed. Kohl steamed on and even became the 'mighty man of Europe' (Time Magazine). Or, to quote retired English minister Wrigley: "German over-confidence rears its head again". This, too, is a German weakness. It is bad for the whole of Europe. For Europe's political and mental health, I hope Kohl will pay for this East German calamity at the ballot box (Subsequent note: That did not happen; Kohl was seen as a hero).

Edouard Prisse

*****

Comment on the above: The second part of my letter is less convincing, but the prediction in the first part was correct, and I never found anyone else who had given this warning. The then president of the German National Bank, the 'Bundesbank', Karl Otto Pöhl, protested Chancellor Kohl's desired exchange rate of one for one East Marks for West Marks, but that warning was only for financial reasons. He did not see the fundamental mistake of giving a strong currency to a weak economy, nor did he see the economic disaster looming. Worse, no professor of economics across Germany saw it, which says a lot about the widespread incompetence that reigned in the profession of macroeconomics! This strange incompetence prevailed roughly between 1970 and 1995 and was later stigmatized by Paul Krugman.[15] It is again rearing its head at the European Commission, since the advent of Ursula von der Leyen.

Anyway, the bankruptcy of all activities really happened, and it has led to great disappointment, anger, incomprehension and, above

---

[15] https://www.nytimes.com/2009/09/06/magazine/06Economic-t.html

all, deep human misery. Many people lost their jobs and were then deemed unemployable by those who came from West Germany with money.

*****

ADDENDUM 2

In 2009, I wrote the article "The Bleeding of Western Power" and submitted it to

the New York Times. They didn't even reply, but the FBI, through a friend, had it on the internet for three years, from 2009 to 2012. So I can at least prove I really wrote this prediction.

You will find this article here. I have taken out a few paragraphs that are now, 16 years later, out of date, e.g., my wish that President Obama would do something about this situation. Otherwise, I haven't changed anything.

*****

An independent view from Europe

The Bleeding of Western Power.

EDOUARD PRISSE, December 2009

Four times, Nobel Prize-winning economist Paul Krugman raised the issue of the artificially low rate of the Chinese currency against the dollar. But keeping the Chinese currency artificially low was only one of three major parts of the picture.

There is also a little history to remember. When Krugman wrote, "If I were the Chinese government, I'd be really worried", *Dean Baker (The American Prospect, December 28) replied that even a gifted economist like Krugman could make a mistake.* Truth is, the Chinese government is not worried at all. It knows very well that, over the last eight years, the odds of international trade have been unfairly stacked in its favor. It wants to keep it that way, and the Chinese will say anything to prevent the still hesitating West from changing this free trade. It is not worry that drives China's policy, it is hard determination.

The Chinese Reservoir

The second of the three aspects to consider in our economic relationship with China is the sheer number of very poor Chinese citizens. Until 2001, such a factor of near inexhaustible, cheap, and available labor in a single country never played a role in world trade. This enormous pool of human resources stands the logic of free trade on its head.

Of the about 1.35 billion Chinese population, roughly 400 million Chinese are now doing well. This number includes millionaires as well as taxi drivers, businessmen as well as housewives, teachers as well as civil servants. The visitor to Beijing sees them everywhere. In terms of local purchasing power these 400 million are comparable to the US and European populations, with the difference that the Chinese incomes are more widely spread.

Less visible are the approximately 200 million Chinese who are poor, but still have a decent roof, reasonable shoes, mostly enough food and often a mobile phone.

But only to be seen by the traveler who ventures outside tourist routes, are the 500 to 700 million really poor Chinese who live on less than $3 a day. 125 million of these have even less than $ 1,25 a day.

We should focus on this "Chinese Reservoir". Information on these numbers varies, but whether the Reservoir holds 300 million or 700 million, its huge size helps China to *continue* competing with other countries at unbeatable prices. This surely pleases the Chinese government, which sees China's wealth increase. But it soon will have disastrous consequences and not only for the West. China's economic power unsettles other countries as well, e.g., Indonesia (Michael Wines NYTimes, December 9th, 2009).

The West believes in the benefits of free trade. The concept has a wide following, and successive U.S. governments have been promoting it with enthusiasm. Free world trade is based on the idea that when rich countries buy simple products from poor countries, the populations of these poor countries will progressively get richer and so can start developing. This allows the richer countries to buy commodities and basic goods cheaply and to concentrate on their own activities at a higher technical level. And as affluence in poor countries grows, this creates new markets. The low salaries will gradually increase, and so the global economy will remain in balance, assuring everyone's well-being. Macro-economically and in practice, this theory is roughly correct. At least, it was until recently.

The Chinese Reservoir has a negative influence on this idealized functioning of free trade. The Reservoir is so huge that the income of its workers, and therefore the cost of manufacturing, does not substantially increase in China and will not do so for the coming 15 years at least. (note from March 2025: It is still not increasing substantially) If a hundred million of these poor should seek higher wages, they can and will be exchanged for another 100 million from the Reservoir. The result is that the inflow of extremely low-paid workers from rural areas and city slums into the Chinese economy can continue for years and years into the future, with costs at bottom levels. This is new in world trade. The total picture is somewhat more complex, but this is the essence.

The effect of the Renminbi pegged to the Dollar and the existence of the Reservoir add up. Together, they violate accepted world trade justification for the first time. Every month, every quarter, every year, China enriches itself with this huge trade surplus income, while the West is being impoverished by the same amounts. In the short eight years since China joined the WTO, Chinese holdings in foreign currency have already become monumental: In September 2009, the total was larger than 2.2 trillion Dollars, a tenfold increase from the already neat 212 billion of 2001. We now see China buying in Africa on a scale not witnessed before. This process is fast, and more importantly, it is continuing.

If this trade imbalance is allowed to continue, and at present signs are the West will let that happen, 15 years from now, these amounts will have changed the balance of power in the world. Not a little bit. Fundamentally. China will soon be able to buy whatever it wants, in whatever domain. It is good to stop for a while and think about what this means. China will not only be able to buy the best researchers, the best companies in the world, and any patent it cares to have, but also the most sophisticated military hardware. China will have no budgetary qualms about increasing its navy fourfold. Moreover, which set of shareholders anywhere in the world owning a valuable asset will not crumble when offered double the going rate? The list is extensive. China will be able to buy real estate of its choice anywhere. And it will be able to buy the loyalty of governments as well as the commodities it wants.

The result: Excessive political and military power accrues to China.

The West will soon not be able to compete because it will be debt-ridden and suffering from diminished purchasing power. In other words, the present imbalance in trade terms makes power bleed from the West to China.

Of course, we must be clear in our basic attitude. There is no reason to begrudge China its growth into a major player in the world. In fact, the West should be happy to see China do what the West did in the last few centuries. That is, we got rich thanks to a combination of good legal and economic state structures and a strong, organized work ethic, not by working for a foreign power at cutthroat rates. The west pulled itself up by its bootstraps. Fine if China does that too and joins the West. There is also no harm in exchanging products and knowledge with China, as long as it is for mutual benefit. But it would be short-sighted if the West continued to allow China's riches to grow unfairly and faster than normal *at the expense of the West*. That is what happens right now.

Mentality

The third factor to consider is Chinese mentality. I have been to China 25 times, and my wife is (was) Chinese. One can like China and acquire a strong admiration for the Chinese people. I do, and I have. But we must also see reality. In China, the spirit of fair play is not in the book, except sometimes inside the family. Fair play is to be found neither in business nor in politics. For the Chinese mind, in the present post-Second World War period, fair play is synonymous with weakness. The Tibet example, although discussed ad nauseam, is still revealing. If fair play were still an element of the Chinese political psyche, Tibet would have been left to its own religious and happy devices during the last 60 years, just as it was by pre-communist Chinese emperors, wisely and fairly, during almost three centuries. The copy of a Tibetan temple, which earlier Chinese rulers erected in Beijing, is still a landmark of the bygone evenhanded mentality of the old Middle Kingdom. The previous rulers respected the Tibetan way of life and showed it,. Since Mao Tse Tung, that fair play and evenhandedness have vanished.

Recently, President Obama displayed a friendly attitude when visiting China. At least, when visible to the press, he behaved kindly. We do not know what he said behind closed doors, but friendliness or, in other words, not talking clearly about serious problems in the interest of maintaining good relations, is not understood as friendliness as the West knows it. It is understood as a weakness to be leveraged against the speaker. We must talk tough with the Chinese while remaining polite as well as strict. This keeps the door open for compromise. Strong and loud language may close the door. Perhaps the President did well behind closed doors; we do not know.

How this started

Many will have forgotten that in 2000 and 2001, China first played European nations against each other and then successfully played Europe against the US. At the beginning of this millennium, in order to be accepted as a member of the World Trade Organization, China had to change a lot in its legal, fiscal, and banking organization. It had to legalize ownership of private property, change its banking system, and accept name and patent protection. Many more demands of the WTO were submitted and, step by step, these were met. As a last demand, after China had already done a lot, at least on paper if not always in practice, the WTO members demanded that China let its currency float freely. Whoever has studied John Maynard Keynes' theory knows that this is a condition to equilibrium. At the time, the Renminbi, also called Yuan, was already pegged to the Dollar. China then lodged complaints, claiming that it had acted in good faith and suggesting that Western countries were just trying to keep it out of the greater world community in which China wanted to become a member in good standing.

At that juncture, something happened for which each European citizen should be ashamed. Opportunistic leaders in Germany and France publicly announced that they would accept China into the WTO regardless of its currency pegged to the Dollar. This left the US as the only strong voice in the WTO, refusing to let China in on this condition. The Chinese government then mounted a superbly executed public relations offensive, stating that the US wanted to keep China out of the WTO, sometimes citing reasons of power play, sometimes suggesting the US was reacting out of fear. China succeeded in casting the US in the role of the backpedaling, dark, jealous opponent. That was at the beginning of George W. Bush's presidency. Surprised and cornered into that position, the US government decided not to harm future relations with China and capitulated.

From this sorry episode, we must remember, first, that Europe was at the origin of the present Renminbi-Dollar problem; second, that a clever opponent can play European countries against each other and against the US. This is the major intrinsic consequence of the fact that the European Union is not a federation but a group of independent sovereign countries, each of which first thinks of its own interest rather than of the greater good. As it happened, the then-German chancellor Gerhanrd Schröder preferred to grandstand against the US. He may also have reasoned that being nice to China would help his country's exports. His neighbor, President Chirac of France, followed suit. The third thing to remember is that the

Chinese have a first-class ability in public relations and in steering public opinion. In this field, they make worthy opponents and should never be underestimated. Finally, fourth, if the West wishes to tackle the problem of the bleeding of its power, it is imperative that the US government succeed in having its major European allies lined up and agreeing before even starting any action. Unfortunately, it remains unlikely that an initiative in this respect will come from Europe. It can only come from the US.

One of the great institutions created by Western society is the World Trade Organization. But now, in the relationship with China, free trade is being put into practice in a way that is fast undermining this Western society. Does the West have the right to change and adapt the rules to this new reality? Of course, it has. Ensuring equality and fairness for all concerned should be considered a first obligation.

China, under Deng Xiaoping, reverted from a communist state monopoly to a free market, individual ownership and competition. One does not forget Deng's adage: "No matter the color of the cat, as long as it catches mice!" Many Westerners were happy to see China join our ideas of maret and ownership when it changed its economic structure. Together with the demise of the Soviet Union, this confirmed that Western society was on the right track. Optimism went as far as Mr. Fukuyama famously writing "The End of History?" For a while, in this euphoria, the sense of reality was lost. After the dissolution of the Soviet Union, the West often thought that Communist rule in other countries would eventually crumble under the appeal of our free society. China was looked at with a benevolent feeling of superiority and President Clinton, during his visit to China, spoke in that sense.

However, from the demise of the USSR the Chinese have drawn different conclusions. These seem to be: Never to let down the authority of the Party like the Soviet Union did. Nip any talk of democracy or dissidence in the bud and use all necessary force or violence to do so. Throughout China, civil servants, personnel of government-owned companies and the huge military are indoctrinated about "correct Party thinking". This is done with obligatory seminars, on average one full week a year and, before important job promotions, for a full month. With this indoctrination, more than half the salaried jobs in China are covered. In other words, the Chinese Party leadership has decided the same will not happen to them.

It is not for this article to discuss whether that is good or bad; the Chinese choose their ways like we choose ours, but we must understand how they view and do things.

The background is also very different from what it was at the Soviet demise of 20 years ago. Unlike the Soviet Union and Western Europe, the two geographies of the West and China are not contiguous. There is no thin and chilling Iron Curtain between them. There is not a whole series of satellite countries craving for their own independence, occupied by force like they were by the Soviet

Union in Eastern Europe. There is no rich versus poor attraction from the West, like there was with the Soviet Union and its East European satellite countries. Neither is there much desire for freedom in China. Living in China, for many, is not so horrible. In short, in China, there is less of a feeling of "Our system is failing" and more of "We are doing better than others, and we will show them."

There is certainly an affinity for our free and democratic societies, and there are some dissidents whose life is made hell, but they are fewer in numbers than in Europe 20 years ago. And in China, there is this strong Party ready and willing to nip dissidence in the bud. Thus, waiting with self-confidence for the Chinese regime to implode is an error. So is thinking that a soft approach to China will succeed. And it would be naïve to believe that everything will come out all right through some natural balance of all matters.

Sidestepping the precise legal aspect, one could say that China is being run under two very different constitutions. Everything that has to do with how the Communist Party keeps its power is inspired by Marxist theory. Everything that has to do with the market and economy, with some exceptions, is being run under the market rules developed by the West. However, in the end, on any decision of importance, the power lies with the Party, not with any market forces. Marxist and Leninist advice on how to keep power is entirely focused on the self-interests of the Party. There is no altruistic idealism of any sort, even though, theoretically, everything is for the benefit of the workers. There is nothing in China's political fundamentals that can be likened to the ideals that one finds so clearly stated in the United States Constitution.

The Importance of Now

Doing the right thing about this skewed situation is now, for the West, the single most important foreign policy issue to be tackled, and it should be resolved successfully in the course of the two or three coming years. This will require strength, determination, and unity of purpose. Astonishing as it may seem, compared to this question and its consequences, Afghanistan is a secondary issue. The war on the Taliban is not putting the position of the West at risk. The Bleeding of Power is.

As recent events have taught, to turn things around, the US and Europe must be able to act together. Without unity, the vital policy of stopping China's unfair enrichment, and stopping the corollary road of the West to secondary status will fail.

Many parameters should be right for this action to succeed, and on a few scores, there are chances. The American President is a capable man. In France and in Germany we see political leaders with a less inward-looking philosophy than before. Both Chancellor Merkel and President Sarkozy are on record for emphasizing the importance of Europe acting with more coherence and unity on the global political scene. The United Kingdom, as experience would indicate, can probably be relied upon to follow a US initiative.

Then there is the Director General of the WTO, Mr. Pascal Lamy. He was reappointed for a second 4-year term on September 1st, 2009 and is now in full understanding of his job. He will be comfortable with its challenges and will have time for important decisions. It is also positive that Mr. Lamy is not an American, but a European citizen: He is French and a good man. There will be European goodwill.

These factors seem to augur well for an American initiative based on the notion of the West as a coherent group with shared interests in major issues of world politics. (comment made by this author in 2022: Here, I have proved to be wrongly optimistic about Mr. Lamy. He has been an idiot instead).

Once the Bleeding of Power is understood, the first question that arises is, "So what should be done?" It would seem a negotiation with China must be initiated towards obtaining that trade flows are equal. This means that the in and outflow of goods and money must be equalized and will have to be monitored so that they stay roughly in equilibrium. This will be difficult to bring about. Many will see this as a step back, and it certainly will be. It is a step backwards in the gradual and necessary opening of generalized world trade. So the question is, 'What is the overriding logic here?' The answer is that in survival, in strategy, a step backwards is sometimes the only right course. Charging forward, blind to the consequences, would be an error. To revert to the macroeconomic sanity that we enjoyed at the end of the last century, there will have to be tough interior adjustments. Wal-Mart and its ilk will have to redirect their purchases elsewhere, and many Chinese factories will have to close.

For China, it will probably be impossible to accept without a good fight the removal of the unfair advantage on which they have already built. The present situation brings China huge riches and global power in record time. We must, therefore, expect China to initially react furiously and negatively. If so, the US, with its European allies will unilaterally have to terminate a number of important aspects of their treaty with the WTO. Given the demonstrated Chinese expertise in public relations, such an action on the part of the West will have to be accompanied by a well-orchestrated, thorough and truthful explanatory campaign to the press and to the world at large.

This must not be seen as an action against China. The aim is to make, maintain and monitor a trade balance that entirely stops the unfair Bleeding of Power, duly executed with the deep respect that the nations involved should have for each other. We will be happy when China gets rich and joins us in a civilized world, but fairly.

Edouard Prisse

*****

Edouard Prisse read law at Utrecht University, received an MBA at INSEAD in France and founded his own company, which had a branch office in Beijing.

ADDENDUM 3

Many denials answered.

Whenever, with friends and others I discuss China's trade advantage and their enrichment at our expense, I invariably receive answers, trying to tell me I am wrong. Although the foolish view that democracy would soon break through in China has finally evaporated, many other incorrect arguments continue to creep forward, some heard as early as 2005. Those denials have diminished a lot lately, but many are still alive. Most of them have a strong component of wishful thinking and are inspired by the desire to remove any unease with a quick denial. Often, too, the denier has an unfounded sense of intellectual superiority, when, in fact, he or she has only read a few newspaper articles.

Here is then a list of those denial arguments with their rebuttal in brackets behind it. I hope this is useful for the reader.

1."China's national debt is about three times larger than their Gross Domestic Product. This weakness dwarfs the supposed strength you describe. China is weak, forget it." (Answer: In reality, measured in the same way, both Europe and the US also have about 300% GDP debt too and Japan has even a debt of 400%. This argument is nonsense).

2. "A huge percentage of loans issued in China, mainly by smaller banks, will never be repaid. These figures are not mentioned, and these banks are artificially propped up. This weakness is a problem for the whole country, and it cannot be

sustained in the long run. The reality behind the scenes is worse than you think. China is really not dangerous." (Answer: This weakness is certainly there, but it is offset by the enormous enrichment that is much greater in volume of money. So, the non-repaid loans do not play a role at all. The thinking error here is a classical one: the speaker forgets the very different economic and monetary circumstances China is in.).

3. "A lot of real estate is built in China, which is then left vacant for a long time. Huge new cities are being seized with the stroke of a pen. In a healthy economy, this would be disastrous., but in China, the situation is artificially protected by the government. This cannot be sustained indefinitely and will implode. We just don't know when." (Warren Buffett also predicted this in 2016. but it still hasn't happened. This is basically the same thinking error as in point 2, only with different words).

4. See here an article in "Foreign Affairs" indicating that Chinese growth is slowing down hard. "Then, of course, export will also decline. You are worrying about nothing." (Answer: Declining growth, even a possible contraction of the Chinese economy, will not reduce exports, because exports are driven by the buyer, not the seller. By the way, this incorrect article was again written by a Chinese person. See Chapter 8.)

5. That new Silk Road through Pakistan? Don't forget how unstable Pakistan is. That project is bound to run into problems. And such a railway requires a lot more maintenance than the ocean liners used now. This project is flawed and will very likely run into

problems." (Perhaps, but does that change the argument I made? It does not.)

6. "They are making mistakes; look at what they are doing in Africa. Already, some countries there don't want to see the Chinese. They are getting stuck everywhere. You worry for no good reason." (Answer: again, even while this is true here and there, that does not stop China's continuing enrichment.)

7. Wages in China are rising now, so many companies are starting to get their cheap goods from other, now cheaper places, like Vietnam. I see that in my work. what you describe so alarmingly will blow over." (Answer: It does not and will not. See Chapter 1. The massive enrichment continues full steam ahead).

8. "Statistics from the Chinese government are unreliable. With that, they maintain public opinion and their stock markets, but that will eventually collapse. They cannot escape reality. You are barking at a non-existent tree" (Answer: I don't use Chinese statistics).

9. "The pollution is getting so bad there that the system will destroy itself. You must realize that it cannot continue like this. (Answer: The pollution there certainly is very bad, but will not stop production).

10. "The IMF has recently said that China is borrowing too much" This argument, as if it concludes all discussion, was given to me by the Dutch former finance minister Onno Ruding. (Answer: The IMF is an advisory organization and a kind of bank, but it does not have any control over the government in Beijing. What the IMF

advises will not happen if Beijing does not want it. And in the above case, Beijing does not.).

11. "History has seen civilizations rise and fall. You can't influence that." (Answer: This sounds grand but is a subterfuge. We can influence trade with China!)

12. "You are basically a revanchist. You want to return to the superiority Europe once had with its colonies. You better look forward; the world is changing." (Answer: It is precisely an aspect of that change that we need to stop. And we can.)

13. "If what you say were true, it would have long been known and discussed. Our world is not so blind. we have intelligent people who really know more about this than you do!" (Answer: People who say this then end the conversation. I have no answer to this kind of argument, of course, except to say that I have indeed examined the situation very carefully and that there is indeed collective faulty thinking and blindness. Just read Clinton's words again.).

*****

"Word of mouth and word of pen are important for a writer. If you liked this book, consider leaving a review at the online shop. Even a line or two makes all the difference and is much appreciated."

*****

www.ingramcontent.com/pod-product-compliance
Lightning Source LLC
Chambersburg PA
CBHW051208120626
46547CB00013B/1259